DANCE ANALYSIS

THEORY AND PRACTICE

DANCE ANALYSIS

Theory and Practice

JANET ADSHEAD

PAULINE HODGENS

VALERIE A BRIGINSHAW

MICHAEL HUXLEY

Edited by

JANET ADSHEAD

DANCE BOOKS

Cecil Court   London

First published in 1988 by Dance Books Ltd,
9 Cecil Court, London WC2N 4EZ.

© 1988 Janet Adshead, Valerie A Briginshaw, Pauline Hodgens and
Michael Huxley.

Distributed in the USA by Princeton Book Co.,
P O Box 57, Pennington, N J 08534.

British Library Cataloguing in Publication Data
   Dance analysis: theory and practice.
      1. Dancing
      I. Adshead, Janet
      793.3
      ISBN 1-85273-003-X

Design and production in association with
Book Production Consultants, 47 Norfolk St., Cambridge

Typeset by Cambridge Photosetting Services

Printed by Oxford University Press

In memory of Pauline, co-author, friend, a fine scholar and an outstanding teacher

PREFACE

The initial ideas for this book came from dance research seminars. The four contributors had pursued postgraduate studies at the University of Leeds under the direction of June Layson, formerly lecturer in dance at Leeds and now Director of Dance at the University of Surrey. They were separately engaged on individual pieces of research and met on a regular basis to tackle some difficult issues that might benefit from the different perspectives each member could bring.

In consequence of these meetings the study group produced an article, 'A chart of skills and concepts for dance' (Adshead *et al.*, *Journal of Aesthetic Education*, vol.16, no.3 (Fall 1982) pp. 49–61) and organised a conference in September 1981 entitled 'The study of dance: structures and issues', at Leeds University, to present the material for wider discussion.

At this point the response seemed to indicate a wide potential practical application and this prompted the group to refine the conceptual structure and to produce examples of the use of the dance analysis framework. The framework as it appears here is considerably modified and expanded from the original version and its theoretical basis made explicit.

The members of the study group were:
Janet Adshead PhD MA (Dist.)
Leverhulme Research Fellow in Dance, University of Surrey, formerly Research Fellow in Dance Workshop Theatre, University of Leeds

Valerie A Briginshaw MPhil MA
Head of Dance, West Sussex Institute of Higher Education

Pauline Hodgens MA
Lecturer in dance and aesthetics, Roehampton Institute and the University of Surrey

Michael Huxley MA
Head of Dance, Leicester Polytechnic

Janet Adshead
January 1987

CONTENTS

TABLES

PART I
Dance analysis: theoretical concerns

Introduction

The book is divided into two main parts. In the first part, 'Dance analysis: theoretical concerns', the major emphasis is on articulating a conceptual structure for the analysis of dance, taking the following notions as starting points: describing the components of the dance, discerning its form, interpreting and evaluating the dance. These notions serve firstly to lay out the many strands of analysis and to locate the basic skills and concepts for the appreciation of dance. Subsequently they provide a tool for analysis, a means or a method for improving observation of what is happening in the dance, identifying the points at which knowledge of a historical or bio-graphical nature, for example, might become relevant, or when it might be appropriate to draw on one's own responses and when to search further in the work for clues about its structure or signi-ficance.

A summary of the concepts involved in understanding dance and the skills required to perform an analysis of a dance is presented in the form of 'A Chart of skills and concepts for dance analysis' (Chapter 6). The 'chart' approach functions as a frame of reference rather than a constant check-list.

The second part, 'Dance analysis in practice', consists of an application of the chart to examples of dance as art. In principle the dances selected for study could be from ritual, social or any other type of dance and, indeed, in the first part examples are taken from a variety of contexts to illustrate this point.

The examples take as their subject matter *Swan Lake*, Act II Pas de deux; *Dark Elegies*; and two performances of 'new dance'. These examples are chosen to illustrate different ways in which this analytic framework might be used and the range of methods and sources on which it draws, in relation to the ballet repertoire, from the classical to the modern, and to emerging styles of the present time.

The nature of the focus in each succeeding chapter is different and therefore a different methodology is employed. For example, in the

1

discussion of *Swan Lake*, some of the many versions and interpretations form the basis of the enquiry in order to attend to the question of what, if anything, remains consistently recognisable as *Swan Lake* over its long history and despite its adaptation by many choreographers and companies.

A more recent 'classic' of the dance repertoire, *Dark Elegies*, is examined through the use of critical reviews of the première and subsequent productions (between 1937 and 1981) to identify changes in interpretation and evaluation of the work. Analysis is used to demonstrate that understanding of the style of a dance must be provisional until sufficient time has passed to assess the extent to which it breaks new ground.

'New dance' in Britain has perplexed many since its emergence in the early 1970s. Questions of interpretation and evaluation are particularly difficult. Whether types of judgement which critics apply to other, pre-existing forms of dance are relevant is one issue that is discussed. Through analysis, however, it is possible to locate the particular and distinctive features of this new type of dance and thus to begin to formulate criteria which are appropriate to the work. The examples used here are from the work of Laurie Booth and Fergus Early.

The final chapter reflects on these issues, draws together the analytic framework with the examples used in the later chapters and opens up the potential application of dance analysis in two senses: its practical application across the dance profession and the areas of debate that remain to be resolved. Although the potential use will differ according to the nature of the interest in dance and the person's role in relation to the dance work – as a dance student, a choreographer, notator, historian etc. – we hope that the arguments will have been sufficiently convincing to demonstrate the relevance of dance analysis.

The contributors to this text have several related aims: firstly to examine the general values of analysing dance works (Chapter 1), secondly to explore the theoretical issues that arise in devising an appropriate methodology (Chapters 2–5), thirdly to arrive at a framework of concepts and skills that might guide and support an understanding of and engagement in the activity of analysing dances (Chapter 6) and, finally, to illustrate by examples (Chapters 7–9) and by further discussion (Chapter 10) how this might be pursued in practice.

In Chapter 1, reasons for the current interest in analysis are outlined in relation to the particular dance educational context from which this development springs. These interests are shared across the arts since dance scholars are not alone in perceiving a need for the detailed examination of artefacts. The shared concerns of the arts provide both a support and potentially similar frameworks from which it is possible to make a tentative statement of what a theory of dance analysis might contain and who might use it. The terms in which such theorising is couched and the languages used to describe dances are important precursors to both the debate on theoretical concerns and the practical applications of analysis and these are briefly discussed.

CHAPTER 1

An introduction to dance analysis: its nature and place in the study of dance

by Janet Adshead

A time and a place for dance analysis
The arts: the need for analysis
The nature of dance analysis
The uses of dance analysis
Language and dance analysis

A time and a place for dance analysis

The impetus for research in the area of dance analysis, for the contributors to this text, came from a sense that the development of dance as a subject of study had reached a crucial point. In the establishment of new academic awards and new courses in dance the possibility for detailed study of individual dances was beginning to emerge.

In 1980 there were signs that dance might be added to the subjects offered in the school-leaving examination in England and Wales, the General Certificate of Education (GCE 'O' level), joining an existing 'Ballet' syllabus. It would offer a new and much broader course catering more readily for the ordinary school pupil's experience of contemporary dance forms. More recently, in 1986, the change to the General Certificate of Secondary Education (GCSE) has produced a number of new dance syllabuses. Furthermore, dance was first examined as a GCE 'A' (Advanced) level subject in 1986, thus offering pupils the chance to study dance to university entrance standard. Significantly for us, the latter demands the detailed appraisal of three dances as 'set works' as well as practical skills and historical knowledge.

Simultaneously, degree courses with substantial dance components which stood apart from any other subject, and which were not necessarily linked to teacher education, had become established in higher education. While the historic association of dance with physical education, and the context of that study within the training of teachers, had provided a framework for the growth of dance in schools in the 1950s and 1960s, the possibility for independence became apparent following organisational changes in the higher education system in the early 1970s. By this time dance had become something of a cuckoo in the nest of physical education, adopting an artistic rationale for its justification, sharing only a concern for the human body in motion and, perhaps, an aesthetic interest, with its host.

In these new degree courses dance is studied in association with other arts (in performing arts degrees) or studied alongside a wide range of other subjects (scientific, historical or social) in two-subject degrees, or within the framework of theatre studies, physical education, or recreation and leisure studies. These degree courses may lead to the award of BA (Hons) or BEd, the latter having as its primary purpose the training of teachers. The first BA (Hons) solely in dance (now titled Dance Theatre), offered at the Laban Centre for Movement and Dance, had begun to produce graduates in the late 1970s, and two further degrees of this kind, offering markedly different courses, have since emerged: the London Contemporary Dance School's BA (Hons) Contemporary Dance, and the University of Surrey's BA (Hons) Dance in Society. (For further information on the range and nature of dance courses within degree structures see Adshead and Hetherington 1987.)

Research into the nature of studies in dance at higher education level at this turbulent time seemed to indicate that while the expansion of dance courses opened up new and exciting possibilities it also exposed the rather shaky theoretical underpinnings of the study of dance (Adshead 1980, 1981). A newly emerging discipline inevitably, and rightly, faces the challenge of identifying its central concerns, demonstrating its methods of procedure and clarifying how achievement in the subject is to be judged. Although the longer history of the acceptability of dance at degree level in the USA is a valuable historical precedent, it is useful as an example only to the extent that notions of education in dance and dance scholarship coincide. There is, for instance, no parallel in the USA with the GCE 'A' level examination.

Outside the field of formal education *research* strengths in dance have long existed in the UK, particularly in dance history, and *training* strengths in the specialist training of ballet dancers and, more recently, contemporary dancers. What the new school examinations and degree courses accepted was the challenge to develop dance as a *subject of study* within the framework of formal education and hence in a manner responsive to the general aims of education. A broader approach than that normally seen in the vocationally orientated training of dancers was necessary and both a more extensive content and a more structured approach than that associated with the Laban-based modern educational dance previously taught in schools.

The concurrent development of research in dance *per se* has been of great value in demonstrating a rigour and depth in dance anthropology and other disciplines applied to dance. Anthropology, history, psychology, sociology, theology – these disciplines have something very useful to contribute to an understanding of the place and purposes of dance in the wider context, illuminating its functions in people's lives. What seems most lacking, however, is a sound basis for making statements that reflect a deep and informed response to *the dance itself* so that its place in life could be more accurately judged.

Arguments about the nature of 'disciplines', 'forms of knowledge' and subjects of study abound in the philosophy of education and it is unnecessary to repeat them here. But it is important to acknowledge the influence of such theorising in clarifying what might be involved in developing dance as an area of study – identifying concepts that are central, describing the procedures that lead to understanding in the subject, establishing principles for the verification of knowledge – these are essential frameworks for the growth of the subject. What is to count as knowledge and how this is to be evaluated is a vital concern, not in order to achieve 'academic respectability', as detractors might infer, but to be seen to be academically *viable* and publicly accountable.

The discipline of dance studies and its central core, that is, the examination of the dance in depth, by analysis, has been slow to develop. The transience of dance is most frequently cited as the reason for this but the growth of widely accepted notation systems and video and film technologies has now begun to make an impact.

Thus from an awareness of a range of somewhat disparate theoretical systems, each asking different questions and getting different answers, but each with justification applied to dance, the most urgent problem seems to be how to effect a change of emphasis to an understanding of the making of the dance and the results of that process – the dances as objects in their own right, to be appreciated for their own sake. It is not the intention to explain the making of dances in terms of the psychological processes of the choreographer's mind but to offer a means of refining the skills of appreciation, skills which are as relevant to the choreographer as to the director, historian or teacher.

The arts: the need for analysis

Although dance scholars are handicapped in analysis by the limited evidence of dances, particularly from previous centuries, other problems exacerbate this. Perhaps most important among them are the sometimes conflicting views of art educators, choreographers and dancers about the values and dangers of 'analysing' art works. These are views that find echoes in all arts disciplines despite much more firmly established traditions of detailed analysis of art works. It is fair to say that the idea of analysis is still greeted with reservations by some 'expert' listeners or spectators in all arts. This may be, perhaps, for the very reason that once the reader, spectator or listener is equipped with some means of access to the work s/he simply engages with it and sees or hears it in all its richness and complexity without conscious or deliberate recourse to specific techniques.

However, if the present position for dance is compared with that of music in the early part of this century, we are forced, by analogy, to accept that a greater richness of understanding is the inevitable consequence of analytical and scholarly study. It is possible to see, in the case of music, just how much of an impact the availability of recordings has had on scholarship with reference to today's record review programmes on the radio and to detailed critical articles where several interpretations of a single work are compared. The result is that performances of a single phrase or section of a work are discussed in depth. Yet in 1909 when Virginia Woolf heard Wagner's operas at Bayreuth she felt that there were immense problems in dealing with this new sound and that these problems arose directly from the fact that the music was heard once and once only. Even in the first decade of the twentieth century there was a wealth of notated scores for study although few recordings. At the present time dance has neither in abundance.

7

> The commonplace remark that music is in its infancy is
> best borne out by the ambiguous state of musical critic-
> ism. It has few traditions behind it.
>
> Woolf (1909; repub. 1979, p.31)

This comment seems strange to readers today when a comparison is made of the quantity and quality of critical writing to which the music student has recourse and that available for dance study. But Virginia Woolf's point is that such critical comment, if made without the benefit of recordings to study, tends to be simply descriptive with little of illuminating insight. She continues by making a comparison, not with dance, but with literature.

> A critic of writing is hardly to be taken by surprise, for he
> can compare almost every literary form with some earlier
> form and can measure the achievement by some familiar
> standard.
>
> (*ibid.*)

Similarly when a new dance form emerges, e.g. post-modern dance, the critic has to be thoroughly familiar with existing forms in order to see how and in what ways the new dance diverges from previous practices and how it draws on them. Being familiar with the varied types of the art allows the spectator to formulate criteria based on interpretative and evaluative principles. It is then possible to make reasoned and reasonable statements instead of making vague noises of approval or disapproval. Virginia Woolf explains the difficulty of making judgements in these terms:

> the fact however that so little has yet been done to lay
> bare the principles of the art accounts for the indecision
> which marks our attempt to judge new music.
>
> (*ibid.*)

In the intervening period much work of this kind has taken place in music, both in the field of musical criticism and analysis of works and in the aesthetics of music, but little in dance. The musical parallel is not without problems. Despite the vigorous growth of 'theory' of music and a fairly strict formal analysis there remains scepticism when the interest is broader than this structural approach. The theory of Heinrich Schenker has provoked a debate that is illuminating for its parallels with dance study. His aim, to link 'theory' in intimate connection with 'art', demands that students should be capable of subtle discrimination in hearing and not simply able to read scores and analyse them. The complexity of the enterprise is illustrated thus:

> the finished work of art conceals within itself countless assumptions – imponderables that demand of those who would re-create with understanding (and every higher act of comprehension is re-creation) a commensurate expenditure of effort.
>
> Jonas (1982, p. xiv)

The assumptions that he refers to are related both to knowledge of music (or dance) itself and to the cultural inheritance that we bring to understanding art; they develop from the traditions of that art and are the means by which art works are able to carry multiple and historical meanings as well as contemporary ones. As Jonas indicates, this makes engagement with the art an active, intense effort of understanding on the part of both the spectator and the performer.

In a new journal, *Musical Analysis*, Adorno points to many of the questions with which we deal in this text but in relation to music. He argues of the experience of the performer (and a direct parallel with dance is obvious) that

> if he does not get to know the work intimately, the interpreter – and I think every practising musician would agree with me here – will not be able to interpret the work properly. 'To get to know something intimately' – if I may express it so vaguely – means in reality to investigate what is essentially contained within the composition.
>
> Adorno (1982, p.171)

The tradition of systematic analysis of musical works seems not to have dimmed appreciation of music any more than the scholar of literature or visual art has succeeded in destroying enjoyment of novels or poems or paintings. Fears that the work would disappear under the miscroscope or on the dissecting table seem unfounded. If there is something worthy of repeated viewing and sustained attention it will still be there at the end of the analytical process. The dance scholar knows this just as the musicologist does, but both would also acknowledge with passion that the only valid *purpose* or

9

reason for doing it lies in the increased understanding and appreciation that may result. To listen to music, to hear its structure and understand how it creates particular effects provides an exquisite delight that using it as aural wallpaper cannot. To watch a dance and see and hear its complex interweaving of rhythms and patterns and to perceive the way in which these contribute to the imaginative significance of the whole construction is, similarly, both the excitement of, and justification for, engaging in analysis.

Criticism, in the form of short articles in newspapers and journals, is a related but not identical kind of activity. It is an important distinction since criticism has different purposes and enlightens different audiences. In literature, music and visual art the practical criticism of the newspaper critic serves the purpose of educating the layperson, the general audience, encouraging attendance at new performances or the reading of new books. The *scholarship* of literary criticism, musicology and art history and criticism serves the purpose of furthering knowledge in each domain and increasing the depth of response that is possible with full knowledge. In a crucial sense it is the vital reservoir from which the general critic works.

A degree of scepticism is to be expected with the development of new theory since theories exist to be challenged for their capacity to illuminate the activity that they chart. They cannot, however, justly be attacked simply for being 'theories' since this is patently what they are. This sometimes happens in the world of art, as though we would all be better off without theories, simply enjoying art works. The problems that would result for appreciation and education if we adopted this line in practice are well outlined by writers such as Best (1986) and Smith (1977). 'Simple' enjoyment and appreciation, it is argued, are the result of hard work, often combined with good teaching. People do not automatically and without guidance find enjoyment in complex works. They *learn* how to do this and are amply rewarded.

Enjoyment and appreciation, however, can take place at different levels and it may be very general, resulting in what the literary theorist Daiches (1981) characterises as 'critical chat', or a civilised exchange of opinion, or it may be much more analytic in character, requiring a rigorous technique of description which directs the reader to the text, in Daiches' case of a work of literature, in our case to the dance.

It should be apparent where our sympathies lie but the sceptic is right to point to the dangers of becoming overly analytic at the expense of engaging with the whole work and responding to it imaginatively. What we want to reinforce is the possibility of giving reasons for opinions, of providing evidence to support an interpretation, of ascribing qualities to the art work and offering some means of judging its value. Only then is there the chance, in consequence of this process, of guiding others towards greater enjoyment and understanding. Promoting one's own views in the name of 'criticism' or 'education' without giving reasons is simply not good enough.

The nature of dance analysis

If we apply these general principles specifically to dance then the notion of analysis has a relevance even at the level of looking at an example of human activity and calling it 'dance'. The perceiver has to have some idea of what a 'dance' is, and this, in turn, depends on having seen people doing something that has been labelled in this way. There are problems, of course, even in *recognising* unusual forms of activity as dance, particularly from cultures other than the spectator's own, and in borderline activities such as ice dancing. A similar problem occurs when the spectator is presented with new forms of dance, whether performed for social or artistic purposes, since they tend to run counter to existing types of dance. They may fall outside accepted or given frameworks and may be less immediately accessible.

For the purposes of this discussion, however, the point is that as soon as someone talks about an activity as 'dance' this is to embark upon analysis, to pick out features of an event and to match them against assumptions about what a dance is. This ability can be refined until the individual recognises the characteristics and distinguishing elements not only of dance (as distinct from drama or music) but of different styles of dance within general groupings of dances and, at the level of individual works, sees the uniqueness of each one.

Perhaps the first and most obvious necessity is to explain in outline what is meant by analysing individual dance works since the term 'analysis' can be understood in a number of different ways. Each successive chapter in the first part of this book explores a section of this outline in greater detail.

The term is used in this book to describe a process which, if

11

sympathetically taught, is crucial in coming to understand dance, to appreciate it more deeply and to value it. Far from destroying the dance it can illuminate it by increasing the ability to discriminate finely between the features of a single dance and to make comparisons between dances. Analysis provides a structure for the knowledge that is needed to frame interpretations and increases the possibility of becoming imaginatively and creatively involved in a work.

Dance analysis does this by taking account, in its conceptual structure, of the movements present in the dance, allowing the possibility of a *minutely detailed examination* of its parts, in the way that a notation score records it, but it also permits a *synthesis* of the results of detailed observation with contextual knowledge, which then furthers the process of *interpreting* and *evaluating* the dance. Dance analysis does not remain solely at the level of a description of movement as 'movement analysis' or a 'movement theory' might; nor is an 'effort–shape' theory (in the sense that some American theorists have developed Laban's work) seen to be adequate to answer the problem of interpretation in dance. The notion of interpretation requires that the character of the dance, its subject matter, the treatment of that subject matter and the qualities that might be ascribed are also understood. This is beyond the scope of theories that simply analyse movement.

Appreciating dance is a complex process which depends also upon the individual having certain skills, for example the skill of noting or observing separate movement components of the dance and being able to perceive them as related or unrelated happenings. Constructing a clear picture of the movements and the way in which they coexist, of the dancers, as individuals and as groups, of the performing environment, costumes and sound, is the basis of analysis.

Once these elements have been seen, and it is often no easy matter to grasp them as the dance rushes by, the spectator can proceed to make sense of them by drawing on all that s/he knows about dances, about the type of subject matter and about the conventions of that art, and engaging imaginatively with it in order to ascribe certain qualities and attribute meaning(s) to the dance. Then one could be said to appreciate the dance. It is not assumed that all dances have specific, identifiable 'meanings' in a simple sense but the term is used more widely to cover the 'significance' of the dance or what it is 'about'.

Making sense of a dance requires, then, that an interpretation is made, derived from a rigorous description of the movement and supported by additional knowledge of the context in which the dance exists. But it is not just the historical or biographical facts of the work's provenance, nor simply the details of the movement and its structuring, but the cumulative effect of acquiring this knowledge and then seeing how these elements are transmuted in the whole. The dance may have a purpose or function, primarily as an art work or as a ritual act or as a form of entertainment, for example, or as more than one of these simultaneously. Understanding the individual circumstances of each dance is crucial to interpretation. Every dance is found in a particular cultural context just as, historically, it exists in a distinctive era and is made, performed and watched by specific, identifiable groups of people. These factors are relevant in understanding the significance of a dance and it is at this point that contextual knowledge of dance, embodied in studies from dance history, sociology, anthropology and theology, becomes valuable. It is worth highlighting here that the theory we outline is not art-specific but is capable of functioning across the many purposes of dance.

To start from direct engagement with the dance in the way we describe in this text is to focus on the dance itself while acknowledging that other forms of scholarship contribute to the total picture. To take an anthropological or historical starting point is to conduct a different kind of study based primarily on the interests and methodologies of those disciplines. Many dance scholars start from such backgrounds and examine the dance as an expression or subversion of certain aspects of society or as part of an important historical event or period. Constructs central to those disciplines then underlie the study of dance.

While a report of a dance ritual or social event, an anthropological study of a dance form or a guide to understanding the historical significance of a dance, may contain important first-hand accounts, they embody a particular kind of interest that influences comments made about the dance. In other words, writings by historians and sociologists are already forms of analysis from the standpoint of the development of dance *through time* and in relation to its *place within a certain society*. The reader needs to be aware of this.

Our premise is that a satisfactory analysis which starts from the dance has yet to be fully worked out.

The uses of dance analysis

If analysis is seen as a close examination of the parts of a dance in order to make an interpretation of it and to evaluate it then this process would appear to be *the fundamental skill* required whatever one's specific interest in dance. The choreographer, performer, critic and notator all work with these same skills and concepts although they do so in different ways. Furthermore, the results of their skills, the choreography, the performance, the criticism and the score are all *understood* and *evaluated* using the same basic skills and concepts. Developing from this commonality, however, additional skills are required in each of the processes of making, performing, criticising and notating the dance. These skills may, for example, be concerned with learning the symbol system of notation, or acquiring the facility with language which a writer needs, or the ability to manipulate movement in the case of the choreographer.

Although it is often maintained that choreography somehow springs fully fledged from intuition, or from unreasoned, inner experiences and that analysis is, therefore, irrelevant, this can readily be shown to be false. From the choreographer's point of view, s/he has to have a clear idea that a dance is being made and not a music piece, or any other kind of object, and this entails a notion of what the dance might look like. Inevitably this is based upon previous dances seen and made by the choreographer. A more or less explicit process of reasoning then occurs. Whether or not the choreographer's reasons for choosing to place one movement next to another are ever made public, or even put into words, we have to assume that there *are reasons*, that making a dance piece is a deliberate human act and not an accident. If the choreographer could not distinguish between different kinds of movements and then make decisions about how they should be placed, linking them to make longer sections in the creation of a whole dance, s/he would not be capable of making a dance. It may, of course, develop along unexpected lines and even the choreographer may be surprised by the result. In looking for 'surprise', artists sometimes intentionally try to escape human logic and the limitations of normal thinking patterns by chance or random methods. However, this is still a positive choice, a conscious decision about procedures, hence a deliberate act. The choreographer is inescapably engaged in an analytic process.

14

It can be demonstrated then that the skills of analysis are relevant not only to those involved in 'academic' studies but also that they are central in making the dance. Similarly, a performer has to observe the differences between separate steps and patterns or groups of steps, between spatial designs and dynamic qualities of different kinds in order to give an accurate and clearly pointed reading. *This involves analysis.* The spectator too, uses the same process although the end product is not a dance or a performance of one, but the enjoyment, understanding and appreciation of it. In a fundamental sense the choreographer and the performer share this spectatorial view of the dance.

Although the process can be demonstrated to be the same, the use to which it is put will vary. The *choreographer* uses analysis to further the end of making a dance, both as part of the creative process and by examining critically what s/he has made previously and what others have made. The *performer* uses analysis in order to improve technical skill and to facilitate understanding of the structure of the dance for the purpose of interpretation. In these two cases the analysis may rarely reach the stage of being put into words since it may be sufficient that it is only partly verbalised, i.e. to the extent that the dancers can pick up the steps and the choreographer explain them. For the spectator who is a casual theatre-goer, or for the social dance participant, the same may apply.

On the other hand, someone who *reconstructs* dances for the repertoire of theatre companies or revives dances from the original notation of the sixteenth or seventeenth centuries needs a much more articulated level of analysis in order to be able to put together the complete dance without the person who composed it being present to clarify what was intended.

The specialist spectator, i.e. the *critic*, uses analysis in order to provide the reasons for an interpretation and evaluation of a dance and to deepen her/his own response. An extension of this is found in dance education where, it is argued, it is only through articulating *what* has been learnt that understanding can be demonstrated to exist. This does not necessarily mean writing scholarly articles. Understanding of the requirements of performance might also be articulated through the *performance of a work* where this demonstrates skills of interpretation as well as purely technical abilities. An understanding of making dances could be articulated through the *composition of a dance*, for example, based on the principles which,

15

through analysis, are found to characterise a particular period. Understanding of dance could also be articulated through *writing* about it. It is perhaps the dance student, or scholar, or theorist who pursues analysis in the intellectual sense of doing it simply for the sake of the knowledge that results rather than for a practical outcome. This kind of study brings with it requirements which may be somewhat different from those relevant to training a performer for the stage. By using analytic approaches, however, any dance student (in the widest sense) may have access to structures and meanings which were hitherto inaccessible.

Language and dance analysis

One of the fundamental problems in the emergence of a new discipline is the clarification of its language. Words take on specialist meanings as subjects develop (some would say they become meaningless jargon designed to mystify interested spectators), examples being found in the many 'closed' language systems used in dance teaching and in some forms of movement analysis. Add to this the specialist vocabularies of the various schools of anthropologists, psychologists, philosophers and sociologists and the problem of understanding what another person says about dance is magnified.

The verbal languages used to describe dance, as with any discrete and developed form of human endeavour, are specialist ones, making distinctions which are useful only to the dance profession and reflecting the conceptual structure of the specific form of the activity. This is not to imply that the use of language about dance then becomes unproblematic or simply descriptive. There are many contested terms in the arts that remain essentially fluid and require imaginative understanding in their application to a dance. But unless there is discussion of terms, and some consensus on their use, communication is at best frustrating and at worst impossible.

We have a special problem with dance. Firstly we have to *create* a 'text' unless the dance is already notated, hence the need for detailed and systematic description that is as value free as possible. Otherwise extreme uncertainty remains in knowing how much to attribute to the performance and how much to the choreography. Only with a text or a notation of the choreography can we begin to distinguish particular interpretations of the dance from each other in any detail.

16

The process of establishing an appropriate language for dance analysis is dependent upon a system for generating clarity in observation and description of typical dance movements. By describing the *exact* form in which the movements occur in particular instances it is possible to pinpoint the elements which are distinctive of that work and of that style of dance. The range of components to be analysed is reduced because each dance uses only a small selection of elements. The language (verbal) which is used to describe this *particular* dance can be seen as a selection from the total dance vocabulary according to the dance style or form – an economical mini-language within the whole. This can readily be illustrated by the shorthand phrases that summarise particular combinations of movements. Terms such as 'pas de basque' become, through time, the verbal currency of one style of dance and encapsulate certain combinations of elements. Subsequently, of course, such terms may be adopted in other styles of dance causing confusion if used to mean rather different things in different contexts. An interesting example of nineteenth-century shifts in meaning can be found in Hammond's (1984) analysis of ballet technique.

Although these terms are likely to have some common meaning throughout the history of dance for both theorists and teachers they will have described rather different movements at different times and will have carried different cultural overtones.

It is notation systems that provide the key to relatively unambiguous communication through the creation of an agreed symbol system. Notation is not totally unambiguous however, in the sense that any system used to notate a dance already encapsulates a description and analysis of the movement as found in a specific context. Evidence for this line of argument is found in the fact that historically *many* notation systems have developed, each primarily in response to emerging styles of dance, and each embodying the characteristics of those styles (see Hutchinson Guest 1984 for a full account).

While this is true to a certain extent with modern notation systems they are also used outside the dance context and seek to record wider uses of movement. Systems for analysing and recording movement which claim universal application have been researched in some depth in the twentieth century by such theorists as Benesh, Eshkol and Laban but the problematic nature of the relationship between the study of *movement* and the understanding and appreciation of *dances* has been largely overlooked.

Notwithstanding this reservation the value of using a notation system lies in the production of a score, the parallel in dance terms to the musical score or the text of a play. The performer, as in any art which proceeds through time, has to make the interpretative statement based on this 'text' or score. Analysing the dance score reveals the choreography and allows the student to distinguish it from any one performance of the dance. The form of the dance i.e. its linear development, can be seen much more clearly in this form than in a live performance.

What remains outside the scope of a notation system (and correctly so since it deals primarily with detail of movement and choreographic structure) is the interpretation of the dance. The challenge to both performer and spectator lies in realising the possibilities that the choreography offers. The dilemma of the notator in this respect is well illustrated in two articles in *Dance Notation Journal*. Becker and Roberts (1983) debate the problem of recapturing the quality (a matter of aesthetic ascription) of the Humphrey works once the movement has been mastered. They stress the importance of understanding the set of beliefs that Doris Humphrey espoused on the relationship between

> Apollonian and the Dionysian states of mind; the Apollonian state being balance, verticality, and stability and the Dionysian state being danger, ecstasy and abandonment.
>
> Becker and Roberts (1983, p.4)

'Fall and recovery' are present not just as physical facts in anatomical terms but as a key to psychological states understood with reference to cultural value systems. Becker describes the subtle, qualitative differences in the occurrence of this fundamental principle across the range of Humphrey's works. 'Effort' (dynamic) symbols are employed on the score but it is of significance that words are also used to indicate the aesthetic qualities, for example, of 'swoon' and 'suspend'. It is not the purpose of notation systems to give the fully contextualised sense of period and style or an ascription of aesthetic quality. Many other sources are needed for this and they remain open to interpretation.

In a subsequent article in the same journal Bissell's (1983) analysis of Sokolow's *Rooms* is written in a much more interpretative vein and relies heavily on the choreographer's statement about the theme, the extensive use of words on the score and critics' comments. The actual notation seems of much less importance, while the significance of the movement is the focus, supported by detailed description:

> the young man seems to be racing, trying to out-run his inner emotions. He appears as a lonely figure wrapped up and propelled by a whirlwind. His movements are condensed, repetitious and small; they are held close to the body. [He] ... beats his right foot back and forth over the left leg ... stands low to the ground with torso hunched forward ... repeatedly swivels from left to right.
>
> Bissell (1983, p.21)

The larger impact of the dance is expressed in terms of Sokolow's concerns with how people can be 'so close yet so far apart' (Bissell citing Hering, *Dance Magazine* 30/4 1956, p.60). The danger here is that the choreographer's account becomes the definitive interpretation. Choreographers may recall and explain their intentions and their processes but they are not necessarily in a priviledged position to say whether they have succeeded in realising their ideas. Indeed, the critic John Martin is cited in the same article as finding this work 'dismal', 'commonplace' and 'monotonous'.

A similar problem exists with the use of other crucial sources in analysis as with a score, namely that of interpretation. Whether the record of dance is contained in a written description or an oral account, or exists on film or video, the standpoint of the person who records the event is a vital factor in the evaluation and use of that source.

A film director's choice of perspective, for example, no less than a writer's, will make a recording a further *interpretation* in its own right, with the potential to differ from the choreographer's intention and the staged version. But the benefits of video are obvious in allowing us to get close to the most vital source – the dance itself, once the possible distortions of the two-dimensional image and the problems of filming are taken into account.

The value of film and video is quite different from that of the live performance since the *same* performance of the dance can be viewed many times, stopped at any point, slowed down and reversed. Comparisons of one version and performance of a dance with other film or video versions are then possible, as are comparisons between different performances by the same dancers, or different performances by different dancers. Critics already do this in their writing but based on repeated viewings over periods of time. With videos cross-reference between performances is potentially much greater.

The dividing line between film or video recordings and what might be termed 'dance-film' is often difficult to establish since the difference may be primarily one of intention or purpose. If both film and dance components are used in combination, a 'dance-film', a hybrid form, may emerge, perhaps using electronic techniques to create movement and dance 'images'. If the film is run backwards and the movements, therefore, are reversed, images may appear of actions which the human body would find impossible to perform. It may be that space and time are distorted so that a performance space no longer exists in the same sense as in a live dance and time becomes artificial and illusory. The video itself then becomes a commentary upon the dance.

Despite the welcome increase in the practice of notating and filming dances in the modern theatre, in historical reconstruction and in anthropological research, few works have been notated in the history of dance-making and both reconstruction and scholarship have to rely upon memory and written accounts. These rich sources of information, i.e. records in the written form of dance descriptions or pictorial evidence, augment analysis and provide certain kinds of insight which do not result solely from viewing a performance.

Accounts of dances, written by the choreographer, a dancer or critic, and drawings and photographs bring their own problems in being open to (mis)interpretation but therein lies the interest also, in the point of view that accompanies, or is built in to the description and interpretation of the dance.

Greater clarity of language and terminology is an essential precursor to the valid use of this range of important sources in the analysis of dances.

CHAPTER 2

Describing the components of the dance

by Janet Adshead

Movement
Dancers
Visual setting
Aural elements
Four research examples

At the beginning of Chapter 1 the statement was made that a dance has separately identifiable components, that it is made up of movements which are performed by a single dancer or by a number of dancers, in a particular setting. These dancer(s) are usually clothed, sometimes in special costumes, and they perform in a visual environment, often with sound accompaniment. Chapter 2 contains an expansion of this statement and, in addition, offers a structure for looking at the components of the dance. These observable features, which can be identified and their existence agreed upon literally by pointing to them, are the substance of Chapter 2.

There are two separate but related aspects of the presentation of a dance, the observable elements or components and a person's perception of them. The components are the main focus here although it is acknowledged that for two people to talk about features of a dance they both need to have seen them. The ability to perceive accurately and in detail develops with practice and this can be facilitated if relevant features are pointed out. The *skills* that are necessary at this most fundamental level of dance analysis are those of being able to

— *discern differences* between movements and among other elements
— *describe* these features and
— *name* them.

The act of naming a movement as, for example, a leap (i.e. a jump from one foot to another) carries with it a recognition of a group of characteristics. The ability to recognise elements grouped in these ways requires the formation of concepts and it can be demonstrated that these concepts have been acquired if the word is used accurately on subsequent occasions. These *concepts*, which are the basis of dance analysis, are derived from the components of the dance and its presentation.

The components which are observable in a dance can be grouped under major categories concerning the movement; the dancers; the visual setting; and the aural elements. The numbers in brackets, here and in subsequent chapters, correspond to those used in the chart presented in Chapter 6.

Movement (1.1)

Each dance genre and, within this, each style, uses *some* of the humanly possible actions of the body, selected from gestures, bends, extensions, twists and turns. These activities may be combined with stepping, running, jumping and falling, which typically alter the centre of gravity of the body and may consequently lead into travelling. Held positions and momentary pauses in stillness are also part of the focus on the actions of the body. While all manifestations of dance can be said to be concerned with movement possibilities, each genre, or particular form of dance, exists as a *selection* from the total range. Within the genre different dance styles reveal *distinctive ranges* of movement. Individual choreographers and performers take and use these styles in their own ways, producing their own choreographic or performance styles.

Hence a ritual African dance may predominantly use small shuffling steps, a social dance of the twentieth century may also use small but metrically rhythmic step patterns, a classical ballet may use rapid running steps. The examples merely make the point that a 'step' or transference of weight from one foot to the other, while being the basic unit, tells us nothing of significance about a dance or a style of dance. The description needs to be clarified, as indeed the above examples already are, by terms such as 'shuffling', 'metrically rhythmic', 'rapid' etc. At different times in history and in different dance forms different kinds of steps have been used.

The selection of particular types of movement is, of course, in the interest of the function of the dance as, for example, social or artistic form carrying certain meanings. The prevailing social or aesthetic norms and current cultural matters of interest may further determine the choice of movement.

To take an example, The Feuillet dance *Entrée à deux*, which Wynne and Woodruff (1970) reconstructed, exhibits vertical, narrow movement with attention paid to the delicate manipulation of hands and feet as characteristic features, thus using quite a small range of movement.

It is often argued that the typicality of the selection of movement is closely related to the motor behaviour of a particular group of people. Kealiinohomoku (1970) found that identifiable traits in normal movement patterns were reflected in dance movement, which is hardly a surprising conclusion but one that serves to reinforce the closeness of the movements of the dance to those of ordinary life in the simple everyday sense in which movement is used.

In addition to the actions described above, there are obvious spatial dimensions to take account of. The moving body has a shape, which may be curved, linear etc., and it has a size, both in its own right and in relation to other bodies or stage or ritual properties. The enormous tower-like structures carried in some ritual dances serve to dwarf the human form. This is itself a spatial metaphor.

In moving *through* space the body creates a pattern both over the ground and/or at different times, through the air. Dance forms use space in a multitude of ways. An Indian classical dancer might use a small dancing area but create intricate patterns within it, particularly in gestural design, while many of the traditional English folk dances (e.g. of Playford) make a positive feature of floor patterning with relatively little design through arm movements.

While the action of any part of the body takes place in a specific direction in relation to the body, whether forward, backwards etc., few dance forms use anything approaching the full range of possible spatial direction. Again, the selection of particular directional emphases derives from the historical origins, purposes and significance(s) of each dance style.

Dance movement also exhibits a *dynamic*. There is a degree of tension or force; of rapidity or suddenness; of sustainment or the extended playing out of a movement. Like spatial elements, these dynamic qualities are also selected from the range of human possibilities; they are found in different proportions in different dance genres and styles. Dynamic 'quality' is often associated with dynamic variety, but the lack of vigorous or notable dynamic *change* is not necessarily a denial of the existence of a dynamic. It is itself a certain kind of dynamic.

Thus a single movement can be described in terms of its action, e.g. a three-quarter turn on one foot; its spatial design, e.g. curved in the body, rotating through half a circle; and its dynamic quality, e.g. forceful or gentle. Hence a movement is not just a 'turn' but a cluster of spatial and dynamic elements combined with a particular use of the body in action. As many readers will know, the analysis at this level of simplicity parallels that offered by Rudolf Laban but similar ideas are also found in many other theoretical accounts of the possibilities of human movement in the context of dance.

These fairly simple notions of movement possibilities in dance might seem facile, indeed, systems of movement analysis which attempt to be all-embracing, e.g. aiming to cover *all movement activities* or even *all dance forms*, tend to give minimal insight into specific dances. All dances have movement, given form in time and space, but the interesting and important part is *what* kind of movement is typical and *how* it is patterned in time and space to produce the distinctive style of a choreographer or genre of dance.

It is pertinent to point out that an anatomical or physiological analysis of movement (of bony or muscular structure and, for example, the cardiac and respiratory systems) is also possible but it is unlikely to be helpful in arriving at an evaluation that relates to the artistic, social or ritualistic purposes of dance. It *would* be helpful in arriving at a statement of the different kinds of demand that various forms of dance make on the body if this happened to be of interest.

To pursue the issues of *movement* analysis further, it appears that any attempt at a global description is not only fraught with practical difficulties but is also unnecessarily cumbersome in relation to the analysis of a specific dance style. However, there has been a substantial amount of work in the USA on these lines. Bartenieff used and developed Laban's effort and shape concepts in conjunction with Alan Lomax's cantometrics projects into a 'choreometrics' system. Her concern was with the search for a means of

> describing dance patterns so that they could be consistently compared cross-culturally, grouped into their re-

gional or functional families and thus studied in their cultural and historical contexts.

Bartenieff (1967, p.92)

One of the main distinguishing features that she isolates is the preference for certain bodily attitudes or postures and characteristic ways of changing from one to another.

Her listing of descriptive components includes

the body; parts and attitudes

transitions

shape

effort

flow

group relationships and formations.

Ultimately, the aesthetic preferences of a society in relation to dance would, according to Bartenieff, rest upon its movement behaviour patterns, and the judgements it makes would in turn rest upon the same premise. However, everyday ways of moving, and the changing bodily positions which are characteristic of a particular society, might seem remote from judgements about formalised dances, and these relationships are merely sketched out in existing theories.

Kaeppler takes the standpoint of an anthropologist and builds a methodology for dance analysis from the isolation of movement patterns but she immediately places these descriptions in context. As she points out, descriptions have to be analysed in a meaningful way since

only a small segment of all possible movements are significant in any dance tradition.

Kaeppler (1972, p.173)

She maintains, therefore, that it is necessary to make an inventory of those movements which are *important* in a particular culture. The methods she employed for doing this in relation to Tongan dance are given in detail in the article quoted above, but they are based on learning to acquire the perceptions of the people whose dance it is. In parallel with the Feuillet researchers Kaeppler argues that it is a question of learning how to think, feel and react as the people who perform or watch the dance would, in order to understand which movements are more important and which less than others.

25

Further general categories of 'dance movement' can be found in Hanna's study of non-verbal communication in the context of dance. The categories that she uses are those of characteristic use of the body in posture, locomotion and gesture space; design, in direction, level, size, focus, shape and grouping rhythm; time and flow, tempo, duration accent and meter dynamics; force, quick and slow, direct flexible and flow. Hanna (1979, Appendix 1).

Her anthropological perspective draws together methodologies from ethnology, cultural anthropology and sociolinguistics with those of physical anthropology and archaeology as a basis for the development of a methodology for studying dance. She applies these theories in a series of case studies.

While there is general acceptance of the strength of some anthropological methods of study *applied* to dance, writers such as Bartenieff and Hanna also argue that the development of a methodology that is *specifically* appropriate for dance is essential. Bartenieff, for example, concludes that

> dance cannot profitably stretch its concepts to fit the mold of existing scientific models.
>
> Bartenieff (1967, p.103)

The basis on which many movement analysts proceed is that of Rudolf Laban's movement theories. His work has been developed in a number of different ways in both Europe and the USA. In relation to analysis and notation, Knust in Europe and Hutchinson Guest and Preston-Dunlop in England have been influential in extending the structure of his ideas. In the USA the development has taken two rather distinct forms, that of notation, through the Dance Notation Bureau and that of effort–shape, through the choreometrics project developed by Bartenieff and others. There has been considerable cross-referencing through individuals and through organisations such as The International Council of Kinetography Laban (ICKL) and the Dance Notation Bureau (DNB).

The categories of effort–shape theory are those of

body attitude
effort
shape

26

spatial orientation
initiation of movement
sequence configuration
phrasing.

Some of these latter categories imply progression through time and are not, strictly, the separate components of the dance. A useful introduction to the use of these systems in conjunction with each other can be found in Cohen (1978) and in Pforsich (1978). Pforsich describes both and then points to ways in which they might together produce a more complete account of the dance. The terms 'Laban-analysis' or 'Laban movement analysis' are then used to indicate that both these methods are being employed. Researchers in this field are attempting to establish a comprehensive movement language which would be valid in cross-cultural research. A recent report on these developments may be found in *Dance Research Journal* (Bartenieff *et al.* 1984,16/1).

Similarly, Kagan, in a comparative analysis of *Three Epitaphs* by Paul Taylor and *Water Study* by Doris Humphrey, argues for an analytical methodology that would parallel the other arts, saying that

> Labanotation alone cannot adequately capture certain stylistic and expressive aspects of a piece. Effort/Shape provides the possibility for making its description more complete.
>
> Kagan (1978, p.75)

Two comments may be necessary here, one is that Labanotation does not proceed beyond the level of describing observable features of the dance, and secondly, that matters of style and expression rightly belong in Chapter 4 and will be pursued there. However, it is precisely in this area, in the ability to account for the interpretation, that the Labananalysis system seems to meet problems.

Theories of composition may offer another starting point and, in the sphere of dance as art, Doris Humphrey's text *The art of making dances* (1959) has been seen as a definitive statement of composition in the early modern dance style. Since she is one of the few highly successful choreographers to lay out a theory of composition it is worth examining the principles that underlie it and the movement components that she identifies. Humphrey expounds her ideas within the framework of the theme or idea, and the appropriateness of different types of themes for dance.

Her theory relies on a fundamental movement principle, that of fall and recovery or balance and unbalance. From this basis she moves towards principles of

design in time and space	dynamics
phrasing	rhythm
group design	words
stage space	music
lighting	sets and properties.

Many texts on ballet reveal similar concerns but a much greater emphasis on set patterns of steps and gestures. A technique text by Guillot and Prudhommeau (1976), based on teaching ballet and on dance history studies at the Paris Opera, offers a clear analysis of the steps and patterns of movement that characterise classical ballet and also gives examples of works covering a long time-span which use particular variations of the technique. Although a more detailed and comprehensive account might be built up by reference to a wider range of literature, the value of this text is its clarity of classification and general accessibility and availability. In the category of single steps the authors identify elements as follows:

placement of the foot, e.g. demi-pointe

turn out

basic positions of the feet I–V

basic positions of the arms I–VII

basic positions of the head.

Clusters of these components produce four kinds of 'arabesque' and two 'attitudes'. Further refinements of all the positions can be found in Guillot and Prudhommeau's descriptions. The numerical possibilities of combining leg, trunk, arm and head positions, from the 47 identified as separate positions, culminates in a total of over 13,000. If the variation in the use of the foot is taken into account, using the flat foot and two pointe positions, then the combinations are over 39,000 in number. This only refers to static single positions at a specific moment in the dance. When the position is changed to another and the transition is described, the complexities increase. In addition there are clusters of movements which have acquired names, either in ballet itself or in other activities such as gymnastics, but which are now used in ballet, e.g. acrobatic movements, 'cartwheels', 'splits' etc. The purpose of quoting this example is simply to point to the enormity of the most basic aspect of analysis, that of describing the movement.

An example of dance analysis from a different genre, that of jazz dance, is found in the work of the Stearns (1964). Their concern is not to categorise all movement but to examine particular styles of dance within the jazz genre. Indeed their examples were selected *because* they use the elements that characteristically determine the form, hence they are central cases. One of these characteristics is the in-built capacity of the style to allow for individual variation.

Although the basic patterns are well established, regional and personal variations are expected. Dances are grouped together according to the importance of specific movements, e.g. steps in different directions; accents in different parts of the trunk and feet; the use of hand, head and shoulder movements. Thus the 'mashed potato' can be compared with the 'chugg', the 'goose neck' or the 'turkey trot'. Notation is used to give a detailed picture, and a glossary of symbols is provided that would allow even a beginner to make a start at understanding the differences between these phrases. It is commonly asserted that jazz dance steps derive from African sources and the Stearns demonstrate through analysis that the central characteristics of the African elements of jazz dance are

flat footed, gliding, dragging and shuffling steps
posture with knees flexed, body bent at the waist
centrifugal movement outward from the hip area
performance to a propulsive rhythm usually provided by jazz music
improvisatory procedure
imitation of animals in a realistic manner.

The latter statement is one of interpretation but in this case the association of particular movements with ideas is very close since the dance is often directly imitative.

The Stearns monitor subtle, changing styles in the twentieth century and the relationship between jazz dance, theatrical dance and other forms of social dance.

Under the heading of 'movement' it is clear that whatever the form or style of dance, the shared concerns are those of a range of action and gesture, of spatial and dynamic elements within a specific band and the progression of clusters of these elements through time.

The significance of notation in analysing the components of the dance is considerable. What it provides is a structure for examining the action of the dance with clarity. Because of the details that such a system demands it has, perforce, to give access to the smallest shift in position. Hutchinson Guest (1983) gives an account which is both accessible and applicable to many forms of dance. It focusses solely on torso movements with notated examples.

Dancers (1.2)

Factors relating to the participants in a dance may or may not be particularly significant in specific instances, but noting their age, sex, size, number and role is part of discerning and describing the components of the dance. It may also be important in terms of the style, purpose and meaning(s) of the dance. It may be obvious from programme notes in a theatre dance or from social status in a ritual one that individuals adopt certain roles and are more or less central than others. It is also clear that while many social dances allow performance by any person others are exclusively danced by people of a particular age or sex. In some dance forms the person's role in the wider social community determines her/his role in the dance. Within the classical ballet and modern dance traditions a very definite preference has emerged for dancers of distinctive shapes and sizes, hence the choice of performer is made with reference to a new set of criteria.

Information of this kind may be partly derived from background knowledge of the dance, its type and function, but it is also obvious within the presentation of the dance itself. It is the dancers, moving in relationship to each other and the other components of sound, set, etc., that give rise to the dance. The elements that are directly derived from the existence of the dancers occur in clusters, that is, a dancer is male or female, of a particular body shape, and takes a certain part in the dance. These simple facts are the base from which one can make statements about the sequences of action that the dancers take part in and, later, of the character, qualities and meanings of the dance.

Visual setting (1.3)

The visual environment or setting of the dance covers the performance area, costumes or clothes, properties of any kind and lighting. A dance may take place in the open air, as many folk dances do, while in contrast a performance may be given on a stage in the traditional theatre with a proscenium arch. The changing shape of the space in which dance takes place may be the result of practical matters or it may be closely related to the purposes of the dance and the statement it makes. Art galleries, parking lots, roofs, walls and lakes have become the backcloth for particular kinds of dance in recent years. The use to which the space is put is also constantly changing since events may be located differently within it. Criteria that govern the design of the dance within the space can be seen to have shifted substantially, for example Cunningham's 'bunching' of dancers would be unheard of in a classical work.

Dances may occur in churches or special ritual places and in social gathering places. The place may be particularly significant in relation to the individual dance. Ballet requires the traditional theatre stage, modern dance is more flexible but normally uses a platform or performance area of some kind while the post-modern or new dance tends to take place in a wider range of environments.

Taking the plaited maypole dance as an example of the use of properties, Judge (1983) points to the importance of coloured ribbons on some occasions and the equally significant lack of them on others. They help to indicate the origins and purposes of different forms of maypole dance. In discussion of the contexts in which maypole dancing was seen in the mid to late 1800s he gives evidence that it was

> a popular attraction in a wide range of public situations, in theatres and pleasure gardens, in association with well dressings and with May Queens, used by Friendly Societies, by Bands of Hope, by clergymen with building funds and by enterprising landlords.
>
> Judge (1983, p.15)

Clothing changed, as did the age and sex of the participants, according to the intentions of those who promoted the dance and the situation in which it was to be performed.

Aural elements (1.4)

Dance is frequently accompanied by sound, although not invariably, and this sound may be random noise, the spoken word, singing, or instrumental music in a wide range of musical styles. The sound may be created in collaboration with the dance, or specially for it, or may coexist or may have an existence prior to the dance. Historically, the dance in many of its forms has relied upon music for its structure and rhythms, particularly in folk styles and classical ballet. The reverse may also be true, that music has come into being because there is dance. In some performance arts, dance and all the elements of sound, design and so on are equally important, while in others, one art may provide the reason for the activity and this then tends to control the structure of the work.

In principle the same range of possibilities exists with the use of words or random sounds. Alston's *Rainbow Ripples* is an example of the random use of words in modern dance. Tongan dance, in stark contrast, is largely an interpretation of highly meaningful poetry.

Preston-Dunlop (1983) examines the spatial aspect of movement in some detail. Using the term 'choreutics' from Laban's work she proposes a series of concepts including the 'kinesphere', a 'geometric model' related to traditional ballet and Laban-derived spatial designs, and 'choreutic forms'. She reduces accepted designs to the simplicity of the line and curve and produces a general statement to serve as a baseline for the addition of dynamic and other forces.

It is of interest in relation to the argument developed here that she also arrives at the notion of 'clusters' and of both simultaneous and sequential progression.

For the sake of clarity each of these elements, of the movement, the people who dance and the musical and visual setting in which the dance occurs, has been described separately. It is self-evident however, that in practice at least two of these cannot occur without each other, namely the movement and the dancer. In addition, there will inevitably be some setting for the dance and possibly some aural components. The simultaneous occurrence of a number of elements is termed here a 'cluster'.

Four research examples

In order to demonstrate the relevance of these general principles to the world of dance, four examples of analysis have been selected. They illustrate the distinctive selections of components described above. These examples, which are taken from pre-existing research studies, apply analytic procedures to a number of different dance genres. The four examples are used consistently through Chapters 2, 3, 4 and 5 so that the progression to an interpretation and evaluation of a dance is directly related to the same dance examples.

In using these studies only the evidence presented by the authors in the named texts is cited. The authors have condensed their original findings for presentation in article form, hence they are not comprehensive accounts of the research (with the possible exception of Hilton's work which is in book form). The selection of extracts for the purpose of illustration in this text is a further contraction of the material and while every effort has been made to remain true to the original the reader is referred to the research studies for greater detail.

Example 1: Step Dancing is found as part of the range of social dances in the context of British traditional dance in the early twentieth century. The research is from

> Hulme, A-M, and Clifton, P, 'Social dancing in a Norfolk village 1900–45'. *Folk Music Journal* vol. 3 no. 4, pp. 359–77 (1978)
>
> Clifton, P, and Hulme, A-M, 'Solo step dancing within living memory in North Norfolk'. *Proceedings of the first Traditional Dance Conference*, pp. 29–58 (1982)

Example 2: Tongan dance is an illustration of the dance forms of a non-European society. The research is from

> Kaeppler, A L, 'Aesthetics of Tongan dance'. *Ethnomusicology* vol. 15 no. 2, pp. 175–85 (1972)
>
> Kaeppler, A L, 'Method and theory in analysing dance structure with an analysis of Tongan dance'. *Ethnomusicology* vol. 16 no. 2, pp. 173–217 (1971)

Example 3: French Noble dance. The Noble style of choreography is found as part of a range of court and theatre styles which were performed in France between 1690 and 1720. The research is from

> Hilton, W, *Dance of court and theatre. The French noble style 1690–1725.* London: Dance Books (1981)

Example 4: Doris Humphrey's Water Study (1928) is taken as an example of her personal choreographic style, within the general style of the modern dance genre, in America in the middle of the twentieth century. The research is from

> Davis, M A, and Schmais, C, 'An analysis of the style and composition of *Water Study.*' *CORD Dance Research Annual I*, pp. 105–13 (1967)

Kagan, E, 'Towards the analysis of a score. A comparative study of *Three Epitaphs* by Paul Taylor and *Water Study* by Doris Humphrey.' *CORD Dance Research Annual IX*, pp. 79–92 (1978)

Although it is the components of the dance that are important here, it is perhaps necessary to explain each style briefly. *Solo step dancing* was one of a number of styles of stepping dances performed in Norfolk. It was a lively, vigorous form of social activity which ceased after the Second World War. Several genres of *Tongan dance* exist but they have in common the interpretation of poetry and/or the creation of 'beauty'. Their significance is both ritualistic and artistic. The analysis of the French dance of the *court and theatre* of Louis XIV's time focusses on one particular style, the *Noble* style. It includes several dance types but the overall intention was to demonstrate nobility, grace and elegance in the acting out of normal social interaction patterns of behaviour at court. One of Doris Humphrey's most famous works, *Water Study*, has been extensively discussed in the dance literature and a movement analysis exists, as well as a substantial amount of criticism. It is seen to typify her style and is regarded as a poetic image of water.

In examining the information condensed into table form (pp. 39–40) it is reasonable to deduce the following:

1. *The range of bodily action each dance type uses is distinctively different.*

Solo step dancing exclusively uses the *feet*, but makes great play of the possibilities thereof. Tongan dance, in contrast, has a detailed articulation of *arm* and *hand* gesture patterns. In the French Noble style it is the *carriage* of the body that is important, with fairly simple step and gesture patterns performed around a fixed, upright bodily stance. *Water Study* also focusses on the *trunk* but it is the use of the full range of twisting and bending movements performed in successive patterns that gives it a characteristic style.

2. *Spatial and dynamic elements further define the specific use of the body.*

The solo step dance uses the most restricted spatial range imaginable, a nine-inch square tile. In other words the dance stays more or less *on the spot* and uses only forward and backward movements. However, the *rhythmic range* is wide since the possibilities for creating dynamic variation within an 8-bar phrase in 4/4 time are vast. Furthermore, the performer makes these choices in performance. Tongan dance uses pre-set *gestural patterns* through the space both close to and far from the body and in all directions. The emphasis on design in space rather than rhythm is already linked with the focus on the arms and hands rather than the feet. The clusters are logical, not random. Strictly prescribed *floor patterns*, or pathways, characterise the French Noble style and the individual dancer is seen placed in an established order. The dynamic range varies with the individual dances but in general it is *sustained* and *calm*, matching or crossing the metre of the music with an even flow. The body is always upright. In drastic contrast *Water Study* employs *eight* distinct *levels* of movement, including a fully prostrate position and jumps from the ground. *Curving* patterns dominate *Water Study* with *dynamic peaks* giving an ebb and flow feel to the dance. The rhythm is derived not from music but from breathing and wave-like patterns of movement.

3. *The number of dancers employed, their sex and role, reflect the function of the dance.*

Any individual could step dance although it was originally performed by men since it occurred most frequently in pubs. Women, however, performed at home and in general social gatherings. The dancers in Tongan dance may be *young girls, women or men* and some dances are performed by one group only. A 'lakalaka', for example, requires between 100 and 200 women and men to perform. They do so in lines grouped with their own sex but all facing the audience. The movements that they perform are different, the men's vigorous and the women's graceful, 'reflecting the Tongan conceptualisation of movements appropriate to the roles of men and women', as Kaeppler puts it (1971, p. 180). The movements in the French Noble style are not in general significantly differ-

35

ent for each sex except in a few special dances. There are *male solos* and *duets for men or women or one of each*. Their roles reflect the social niceties of courtship and good manners in the early eighteenth-century mode. Although performances of *Water Study* have normally required *11–16 female dancers*, an African reconstruction used men only (Cook 1977). The reasons are not to do with the dance as such but with attitudes towards dance on the part of men. There are no solo roles, it is a group dance where each individual is subordinate to the artistic expression of the whole.

4. *The visual setting provides the climate and immediate context of the dance.*

Solo stepping might be performed *anywhere*, outdoors or indoors, as long as the floor was hard. Wood or tiles were carried around for the dancing surface so that impromptu dancing could occur. *Clogs* were the traditional footwear. Tongan dance performers have rigidly assigned positions within the lines of the dancers. *Lines, and placings* within them, reflect the dancers' social status, which is derived from a complicated set of relations to the chiefs. In the French Noble style a similar hierarchical principle determined who danced where in the *rectangular enclosed space*. The 'presence' at one end formed the *focal point* and the dance related to this. The ornate, tight, heavy costumes reinforce the uprightness of the carriage of the body. In contrast, the dancers in *Water Study* are virtually naked, *flesh-coloured leotards* being the usual costume. Performing spaces vary and rarely are props or backcloths important. *Lighting* effects, a feature of twentieth-century theatre, are employed to enhance the image of water.

5. *The dances are related to sound or the lack of it.*

In all four instances, sound of some kind, or the absence of it, is important. *Hornpipe* tunes played on a variety of instruments provide the rhythm to play with, and against, for the step dancers. The Tongan dance is essentially an interpretation of *poetry* or formalised speech which accompanies it, often in *sung* form. *Set musical forms* are crucial for the French Noble style since musical and dance forms developed together in this period. In contrast, *Water Study* has *no* sound accompaniment. In its first performance a gong was used but subsequently the dancers have relied on a sense of non-metric surging rhythm which comes from the movement itself, in breathing.

The ability to discern, describe and name the components of the dance, its movements, the dancers, the visual and the aural setting, is the most basic and fundamental of the skills required in dance analysis. The importance of this stage cannot be stressed too strongly since it is only by reference to the observable features of the dance that its structure can be pinpointed. The next step is to understand how these elements are combined in the passage of the dance through time. Only then can a valid interpretation be made and an evaluation formed which can be fully justified. The skills required for discerning, describing and naming components of the dance have to be acquired through patient study.

Table 1. Four research examples: the components of the dance

STEP DANCING: HULME, A-M, and CLIFTON, P, 1978
CLIFTON, P, and HULME, A-M, 1982

COMPONENTS OF THE DANCE

1.1 *Movement:*
    'tap' beat made by ball or toe striking ground
    'step' beat made by ball or toe striking ground and taking weight
    'heel drop' heel lowered
    'hop' and 'spring' rising off ground, landing on same or other foot respectively.
    shuffles and heel clicks

    1.11 *Spatial elements:*
        size of step small
        direction forward or backward
        location on the spot

    1.12 *dynamic elements:*
        strong and fast action
        8-bar phrases in 4/4 time
        unlimited number of phrases

1.2 *Dancers:*
    a single dancer, male or female, or two performing simultaneously or consecutively
    audience essential

1.3 *Visual setting:*
    public houses or social gatherings in the home
    clogs worn on the feet
    dance performed sometimes on a 9″ square tile

Table 1 – *continued*

1.4 *Aural elements:*
music in hornpipe style played on a variety of instruments, e.g. accordion, melodeon, one-string fiddle
8-bar phrases in 4/4 time, quavers divided into semiquavers and triplets making complex mixtures of rhythms
1.5 *Complexes*
upright, solo dancer using part of the foot in metric beats

TONGAN DANCE: Kaeppler, A L, 1971
Kaeppler, A L, 1972

COMPONENTS OF THE DANCE

1.1 *Movement:*
use of legs, arms and head, 1 specific movement of the head tilting to the right; 11 types of leg movement including knee bends, kneeling, crosslegged sitting, turns and travelling steps; complex arm movements involving rotation of lower arm, bending and flexing of the wrist; 6 finger positions, 17 arm positions; touching and
brushing actions; facial expressions

 1.11 *Spatial elements:*
 directional use of forward, backward and sideways movement in both arm and leg action, movement close to and far from the body
 patterns in lines
 small and large steps

 1.12 *Dynamic elements:*
 accents
 greater and lesser degrees of strength

1.2 *Dancers:*
young girls, women, men
some patterns restricted to one sex
there may be variation on a basic position according to the sex of the dancer

1.3 *Visual setting:*
women's clothing tightly wrapped from waist to knee
young girls and men's looser

1.4 *Aural elements:*
three types of hand claps
finger snapping
music
poetry

1.5 *Complexes*
typical position, legs flexible at knees, moving to front, back or side, with emphasis
in lower arm movement held close to body, performed by a dancer who is male or female

---

FRENCH NOBLE DANCE: Hilton, W, 1981

COMPONENTS OF THE DANCE

1.1 *Movement:*
carriage of the body; head upright, shoulders back, arms by the side and slightly away from the body, feet turned out to 45°
steps with weight on ball of foot, sink, rise, spring, slide, turn
movements of the hand, arm and head

Table 1 – *continued*

1.11 *Spatial elements:*
arm movements usually small in size and in the range upward/downward, inward/outward, describing circular pathways

1.12 *Dynamic elements:*
metric patterns dominate in conjunction with the dynamic range appropriate to each particular dance, qualities range from strong to light and from rapid to sustained.

1.2 *Dancers:*
men only
women and men together
duets for two women or two men

1.3 *Visual setting:*
stage space rectangular, deeper than wide, with focal point at one end where the 'presence' is
ornate costumes specifically designed, with effects on body carriage, from heel height; arm position from width of skirt

1.4 *Aural elements:*
music, use of set forms
triple time, e.g. sarabande
duple time, e.g. bourrée, gigue

1.5 *Complexes*
dynamic emphasis within the movement appears with the musical emphasis on the first beat of a bar or deliberately placed against it.

WATER STUDY: BY DORIS HUMPHREY:
DAVIS, M A, and SCHMAIS, C, 1967
KAGAN, E, 1978

COMPONENTS OF THE DANCE

1.1 *Movement:*
all movement related to the centre of the body arching of the back, twists in the torso, arc-like gestures, jumps, rolls, slides
travelling step patterns
whole body extending and shrinking from hyper-extension to complete folding
successive movements pass from the toes, through the knees, hips and spine to the top of the head.

1.11 *Spatial elements:*
use of eight distinct levels from lying flat on the floor to jumping away from it
curving and strength line patterns on the floor
two characteristic designs, a wheel pattern leading into a somersault, another circular pattern horizontally around the body
random scattering of the group and close group formations

1.12 *Dynamic elements:*
six stages along a continuum of degrees of flow identified
variation in dynamic from fast to slow making marked accelerandos and deccelerandos
rhythm from the natural phrasing of the wave-like movements in breath rhythm

1.2 *Dancers:*
different performance accounts list between 11 and 16 dancers
with one exception, all female dancers are used

Table 1 – *continued*

1.3 *Visual setting:*
   variable between performances but rarely any stage props or special costume
   most usually flesh-coloured leotards
   occasional use of blue cellophane backcloth and floor covering

1.4 *Aural elements:*
   first performance used a gong softly giving a beat, subsequent performances no
   metrical accompaniment

1.5 *Complexes*
   a typical grouping of elements would contain a dancer's body in profile as part of a
   larger design of the group with spatial tension evident.

NB Variations occur, e.g. in the Travellers' stepping, gypsy music is used, in the Lancashire stepping, ordinary leather shoes are worn but the traditional Norfolk stepping is taken here as the basic form.
© Adshead, J, adapted from authors' accounts.

CHAPTER 3

Discerning the form
of the dance

by Janet Adshead

In Chapter 2 fundamental skills of discerning and describing the separate, individual features of the dance and of naming them are outlined. The skills of discerning, describing and naming are the basis also of the second stage of analysis but here they are applied to the form of the dance, to matters of structure and relationship. The same type of skill is required but the emphasis is on the nature of *relationships* between components of the dance and not on the nature of the components themselves. It is relationships *between* components that bring about structure, hence the movement and other elements of a visual and aural nature are manipulated and put together in particular ways to create a form. Specifically, the relationships are created by movement in time and space in association with visual and aural materials. Relationships may exist within a single movement and between one movement and the next, one dancer and the next, etc.

Many of the basic 'units' of a dance style (as described in Chapter 2) already contain notions of form in the sense that they appear in *collections* of elements which make a distinctive pattern, e.g. a pas de basque step, or a travelling design over the floor. These 'units' are often characteristic of a dance style. Some will be found in a single dance but others recur and are the clue to broader categories of dance style.

In the *making* of a dance the choreographer works on the movement and other elements with the possibility of many kinds of relationship arising within the context of the total conception. As the work progresses the possibilities are gradually reduced and refined. Progression through time is created in consequence of the manner in which the movement elements are manipulated with dynamic, spatial and rhythmic emphasis. In turn, the character, quality and meanings of the dance are made evident. Because dance proceeds through time it has, of necessity, a 'time design', just as its 'spatial design' results from its visual form. For the maker of dance these are basic considerations which derive from the medium. Similarly they are evident in notated scores and in writings about dance. Examining the form of the dance in totality is difficult. The score represents the only means of holding the whole dance still since pieces of paper can be compared in a way that a video recording of different sections cannot. One section of a dance can be placed next to another for detailed visual comparison (see Jordan 1981/2 on the use of score analysis). This makes analysis considerably easier.

In *performance* these relationships are brought into being in a plastic, three-dimensional sense. Performance is the means through which formal relationships are exhibited and interpretations offered. Those involved in the performance, notably the performers, have to perceive that sections relate in certain ways in order to give appropriate emphasis to the movement. The director or reconstructor also has to have a strong grasp of the overall structure and a sense of its balance in order to make meanings evident.

When the character of the relationships has been clarified, the comparative importance of different parts of the dance can be assessed. This is crucial both for the performers' interpretation and for the spectators' understanding since sections of the dance may contribute differently to the meaning(s) inherent in the work. Perceiving the structure of the dance is of obvious importance for *appreciation*, whether this is by a casual spectator or the professional critic. The ability to note sections of the dance and retain them in the memory as the dance continues to move through time is a skill which can be developed with practice. Knowing *what* to look for must help in this. Thus pointers to the kinds of groupings of elements which are characteristic of a certain style of dance can increase perceptual skills in discerning the structure of the dance.

Just as different dance genres and styles use only some of the total possible range of bodily actions, dynamic and spatial elements (Chapter 2), so, too, they tend to organise movements in a distinctive manner, that is, to link them together in particular ways.

A number of theories of dance structure are described in this chapter, following the pattern of Chapter 2 and using the same sources, but now to examine the use of components in the creation of a structured whole. The research examples used as illustrations in Chapter 2 are carried forward into this analysis of structure.

In the movement analysis which Preston-Dunlop derives from Laban's theories the component analysis is worked out in greater detail than that pertaining to the form of the dance. This may be because the potential range is so large and the selection of structure so dependent upon the style of and genre of the dance. However, in Preston-Dunlop's (1963, 1980) expanded version of Laban's theories there is no particular style referred to and relationship types inter-mingle, e.g. 'combinations of the five body actions' (through time); 'spatial progression and spatial tension' (exhibited in changing positions); 'transitions between basic effort actions' (dynamic change). The chapters which focus specifically on relationships are either concerned with how people relate, i.e. with processes or interaction, or with group design, e.g. 'adaptation to a partner', 'group feeling and group composition' or 'group formations'. Where time, space and weight relations are specifically examined, the range of structures covered by 'synchronisation', 'formations' and 'consoli-dation' is described. Preston-Dunlop isolates time structures which result from the longer span of the dance such as the music-derived forms of binary, ternary, theme and variations, rondo and canon. Spatial forms which progress through time are found in Laban's choreutic theories and these structures produce a complex patterning which carries effort implications and correlations (see Laban 1966).

Davis and Schmais (1967) identify five important structural aspects within the Labananalysis framework. These are analysed in transitions between

spatial levels
shape-flow movement quality
effort-flow movement quality
group relationships
group formations.

This was derived from the effort–shape system of analysis established earlier by Bartenieff among others, and subsequently refined by

Pforsich (1978). Bartenieff's analysis of 'Dance styles in primitive cultures' used a framework for movement analysis which identified specific spatial transitional movements as follows:

simple reversal
cyclic
angular
curved
rotational
looped.

Effort and flow analyses are also used. Bartenieff calculates the relative presence or absence of certain defined transitions from filmed material and places the emphasis on 'ordered cluster(s) of qualities' (1967, p.93). She regards the type of transition between them as an indicator of style rather than deriving style from the character of the separate movements.

In contrast, the main thrust of Humphrey's theory of dance composition is the structuring of whole dances, i.e. giving them form, hence its relevance here. The title, *The art of making dances* would underline this assumption. The major part of the text is concerned with principles of 'craft' and 'design' in dance, based on

spatial design – with a focus on symmetry/asymmetry in body design, between bodies and groups and the stage space.
time design – with a phrase or unit as the basis
dynamic and rhythmic design.

As adjuncts to the dance performance she considers elements such as words, music, sets and props.

The structure of the dance, as distinct from these overarching questions, is the subject of a separate part of her book and for this purpose she identifies musical forms (e.g. ABA); narrative forms; recurring themes and variations; the suite and 'broken' form. The character and quality which arise from the use of different types of movement, shaped and given dynamic stress, are clearly spelled out in the 'craft' section.

What emerges from Humphrey's account is a distinctive range of movement which is coherently linked to a particular notion of the aesthetic in dance. It allows her to produce 'right' and 'wrong' diagrams, so strong are the criteria for 'goodness' within the system.

A good dance, then should be put together with phrases, and the phrase has to have a recognisable shape, with a

44

beginning and an end, rises and falls in its overall line,
and differences in length for variety.

Humphrey (1959,p.68)

Form is seen under a particular aesthetic description and the
movement and other elements selected to achieve this purpose are
consistent with her view of a dance aesthetic.

Although the possibilities for an analysis of formal structure are
immense, they can be simplified for general purposes under the
following headings which derive from the movement components
and their existence in time and space:

Relations according to components (2.1)
Relations at a point in time (2.2)
Relations through time (2.3)
Relations between the moment and the linear development (2.4)
Major/minor/subsidiary relations (2.5).

Relations according to components (2.1)

Any of the components described in Chapter 2 may be traced
through a dance and the relationships which exist between the
movement, the dancers, the visual setting and the aural elements
noted. The repeated use of a jump, for example, or a gesture, a
distinct shape or line of the body, a rhythmic pattern, lighting effect
or a sound element, can be followed. Similarly its performance by
the same or different dancers within the dance, or its varied placings
on the stage, can be described.

As an exercise in increasing perceptual abilities this might be
extremely useful, while as part of an analysis it is highly important,
since *repetition* or *change*, once a framework has been set, is a clue to
the emerging form. A sub-set of this type of analysis would be the
tracing of relationships between different aspects of the *same kind of
component*, e.g. between different kinds of jumps as they appear
through the dance, or the relationship between *two types of movement
components*, e.g. a named gesture and a turn. The emphasis here is on
the components and the ways in which they are juxtaposed.

Wynne and Woodruff's reconstruction of Feuillet's *Entrée à deux*
(1970) is relevant at the level of examining relationships. Correlat-
ing the arm movements with the step pattern provoked much
discussion and proved to be a major problem in determining the

45

structure and style of the dance. In addition, the steps, e.g. a demi-coupé, could be danced in either duple or triple time, which affects the rhythmic quality and overall style of the dance. When this potential for variation in interpretation is added to the variable of the speed of the music, then the range of possible formal structures and hence of performance style is extended. Analysing dance structures is never quite as straightforward as in music, where scores and alternative recordings exist. These developments are of recent origin in dance study. It should be noted, however, that variations in interpretation are in part *dependent* upon decisions concerning the overall speed, the rhythmic patterning of the steps and the placing of arm movements in relation to the steps, that is, on the *relations between components through time*.

However, methods of resolving these questions fully rely heavily upon a wide socio-historical grasp of the purposes that the dance serves in the context in which it appears, as well as on an understanding of its overall quality and its social or artistic meaning. A link is thus established with Chapter 4 where these concepts relating to the interpretation of the dance are discussed in greater detail. It is clear that these stages of the analytic process overlap in order to inform decisions about reconstruction and performance. The performer, as well as the historian, is inevitably caught up in these debates and may act in some sense as arbiter in the choice of detailed movement. A lucid account of similar problems in the reconstruction of Fanny Elssler's *Cachucha* and in the performer's choice of movement and style is given by Hutchinson Guest (1981, Appendices A and C).

Relations at a point in time (2.2)

By 'freezing' the dance at a particular moment it is possible to analyse the visual impact of sets of complexes or components as they occur. In practice this requires photographic or video reproduction or the analysis of the score.

The principle, however, is of looking at relations at a point in time and this can be extended into a 'frame by frame' analysis of the successive moments that make up the dance. In a single moment, relationships across the components will be evident, and it is then possible to classify this occurrence as being of a certain type and 'name' it before comparing it with others.

In the specific case to which Kaeppler (1972) refers, i.e. Tongan dance, the relationship between *actions* and *spatial components* is of greatest interest. Some recurring arm movements are always performed with the arm in a set, spatial, relationship to the body, while other arm movements appear in a variety of spatial relationships. On occasion, movements of the head may be substituted for hand movements. Where a set pattern is performed by both men and women there is a change of emphasis, for example the female performer has greater flexibility of the wrists. Directional placing of the palm of the hand is also varied within four possible positions. In this style of dance there are particular positions which function to mark the beginning or end of sections, i.e. to divide the dance into phrases or time sections. These phrases are recognisable in consequence of the individual moments that make the total.

Kaeppler's (1972) inventory of those units of movement which are significant in Tongan society includes analysis of the ways in which the components are combined in any one instance. The timing of the movement is not a significant characteristic in the dances that she analysed since it may vary while the meaning remains constant. There is evidence, however, of a multiplicity of 'set' patterns which *cannot* be disturbed without losing the meaning. The parallel with a language is obvious and is reinforced by the fact that many of these dances are evocations of poetry. The rhythmic pattern and progression through time is clearly expressed in the following example in which the dependence upon precision in individual moments is evident:

1. Fingers begin to flex or bend (this flexion starts with the little finger), the index finger is the last to bend and does not bend so far.
2. When fingers are almost at kineme F3 (an identified position) the lower arm begins to rotate while the fingers complete their flexion and the wrist moves to W1 (an identified position).
3. Immediately upon finishing the lower arm rotation, the fingers open to F1 with an accent while the wrist moves back to its central position.
4. On completion of this sequence the lower arm rotates in the opposite direction, bringing the palm facing back to the position in which it began.

Adapted from Kaeppler (1972, p.187)

Relations of the hands, circling each other and rubbing or brushing the backs of the hands together, produces patterns through time, which allow the isolation of likenesses and differences in positions at specific points in time.

As one looks at the clusters of related elements it is possible to characterise them as 'simple', when relatively few elements are related, or as 'complex', with many elements present. The likeness or commonality of elements might be the feature that creates interest or, in contrast, it may be differences that arrest attention. The examples presented later illustrate this.

Relations through time (2.3)

Here the focus moves to the structure of a dance in a larger sense of progression throughout the work. Sets of relationships among the components produce units which develop into phrases and sections. These units, phrases and sections become the subject of examination and their re-appearance, in part or in entirety, their adaptation and the introduction of new material within them, are part of building the dance. Names have been coined or borrowed over the years to describe some of the many types of progression through time, e.g. canon, fugue, ostinato etc. Within this overall patterning specific devices are commonly used to manipulate the dance material: elaboration, inversion, repetition, recurrence of some element, alternation of one idea with another, addition of material, subtraction of a phrase within a previously seen section and alteration of parts or of the order of events.

Historically, the association of dance material with musical material and the closeness of the formal relationships has been a consistent feature of their joint existence. This is often, although not always, relevant in considerations of the overall form of a piece. In a discussion of Humphrey's dance *Brandenburg Concerto*, Jordan points to some of the complexities of this relationship. For example, in the first movement of the *Brandenburg Concerto*

> Humphrey treats the opening six bars of musical material differently each time they occur, with slight or considerable variation. This material returns nine times altogether, usually stated twice each time. In the music, according to ritornello form, this ritornello material

appears in different keys and with different orchestra-
tion. But it is recognisable each time; similarly the
reference to the first version of the main dance theme is
clear every time.

Jordan (1981/2, p.51)

Similarly, but at the level of rhythm rather than overall structure,
the propulsive nature of jazz rhythms is held partly responsible for
the rhythmic structuring of jazz dance. Chilkovsky maintains that
the recurrent impulses result in

a continuous stream of overlapping sequences subtly
woven into the gross design.

In Stearns and Stearns (1964, p.421)

She groups individual dances together according to their predominant emphasis on certain movement characteristics (i.e. by movement selection) and then analyses the patterns. Their representation
in Labanotation allows the pattern to stand out on the written score.
Repetition of relatively simple steps and gestures, using first one side
of the body and then the other, gives a symmetrical design despite
the improvisatory nature of the form.

In Kagan's (1978) analysis of the dance styles of Humphrey's
Water Study and Taylor's *Three Epitaphs*, the unit under examination
is a recurring but distinctive phrase from each dance. Although the
analysis reveals stylistic information based on components, it offers
little of a 'through time' account except within the chosen phrase.
Relations between complexes are fully described, e.g. a series of
movements which are repeated but accompanied by different spatial
components. Statements about the relative importance of certain
moments, even within a short phrase, lead the author into interpretative statements. The nature of the analysis employed (effort–
shape) inevitably emphasises particular aspects of the dance and
this is evident in the choice of the following five most important
parameters:
spatial levels
shape–flow quality
effort–flow quality
group relationships
group formations.

Pforsich (1978), using a similar analysis, moves from the identification of movement characteristics to how these elements are

49

organised and patterned. 'Ongoingness' or 'fluency' is the basis of this system so it might be expected that continuity through time would be an important category. The notion of 'sequence and configuration of change' specifically identifies movement through time, with two related notions mentioned, those of simultaneous and sequential movement.

Within a well-established, complex and clearly structured style of dance, ways of making transitions between movements and types of progression through time are likely to be as tightly organised as the steps themselves. Thus Guillot and Prudhommeau (1976) develop the analysis of basic positions into movement through time, to produce categories which are extensive and comprehensive. The two major groups are of patterns which remain on the spot and patterns which travel. In both cases it is possible to identify relationships between movement components precisely, through statements such as:

'remain in contact with' (parts of the body with each other, or the floor in a particular movement, e.g. dégagé):

'remain the same' (in line or extension, one part with another in its distance from the body).

The element that is varied from a constant position is clearly stated, i.e. it is the distance of the working leg from the ground that constitutes one of the variable and distinctive features between the dégagé and the battement (a spatial consideration) while the other components remain the same.

There are many possibilities derived from these two categories, for example:

non-travelling
dégagé
battements
rond de jambe
developpé
fouetté
travelling
marche
pas de bourée
chassé
glissade
pas de basque

The use of the arms and their relation to the steps is also well defined, for example, in the bourrée, a complete body design is evident, giving rise to highly specific relationships of components at a point in time. The subtraction or addition of one or more small components is a common means of altering a basic step in ballet. The subtle differences in repetition make a development in the time structure which is of paramount importance. Reversing the order of events is also frequent, for example, steps which start with a foot in front are then repeated starting from behind. Many modern dance techniques use similar devices both as technical exercises and within dances. It is these slight variations on simple steps which produce particular expressive styles, for example the pas de bourrée sur la pointe is characteristically found in the late nineteenth-century Italian classical style.

When the possibilities of turning and/or leaping are combined with the non-travelling and travelling steps identified so far, as in enchainments, the variation in progression through time is increased further. The juxtaposition of specific leaps and turns with the positions described in Chapter 2 provides an ideal example of minutely detailed construction of named relations, progression through time and also of relations between the moment and the linear development since they are often contained within a set phrase. Each new concept, e.g. 'turn', brings a further set of characteristics, which are added to existing possibilities in a seemingly endless permutation of components.

The arm positions and movements are, potentially, infinitely more numerous than those of the legs but here the aesthetic of classical ballet controls the kinds of relationship that are desirable between the parts of the body and in the progression through time. The tendency towards linear, elongated design and symmetrical harmony of the classical style decrees its form. Some of the complex arm gestures in classical ballet, however, are symbolic or mimetic in character and may not be directly related to the leg movement. Hence the link with interpretation since the components and their relations may be derived from everyday movement, which has 'meaning' in a fairly literal sense, or from the actions of human and animal creatures.

Perhaps the ultimate statement of relationship in classical ballet is the adagio, a set of movements in a slow tempo, performed either as a solo or as a duo. It epitomises all the categories of relationship that we identify here and leads to statements of particular quality and character.

Relations between the moment and the linear development (2.4)

Expressions indicating that some moment of the dance is particularly important are commonplace in dance criticism. Here the impact of a set of relations at a moment in time is felt within the continuing development of the dance. The reasons that justify these statements are the concern of this section, i.e. relations between the moment and the linear development of the work. The existence of emphasis, through accentuation of a phrase, or indeed the marked absence of dynamic emphasis, might cause attention to dwell. Repetition of a movement or, conversely, the introduction of startlingly new material may also highlight a phrase, perhaps through spatial factors in the design of the piece, in culmination of preparatory phrases, or in contrast to what has gone before. In many traditional forms the gradual build up to a climax at the end of a piece is evidence of the importance of a single moment within the total framework. But this is not to assume that the only type of structure which is relevant here is of this kind. It may well be the *absence* of such definite landmarks which forces more careful attention to the whole and to *each moment* as it passes.

Major/minor/subsidiary relations (2.5)

The separate types of relations identified so far, that is, according to components, at a point in time, through time, and between the moment and the linear development have been separated for the sake of clarity of observation and analysis. They are not, however, all independent of each other but are themselves related since a cluster of components, or some part of it, may then be used again as the dance proceeds through time. It is also the case that a cluster can be seen as a high point in the linear development of the work or as a relatively insignificant transitional movement. At this level of analysis the complexities and permutations of possibilities produce the *total web of relations*.

There are a number of possible and valid ways of examining the total web of relations that make a dance. The decision about which perspective and method is relevant and appropriate in each case is dependent to some extent upon factors concerned with interpretation. Although these are dealt with in Chapter 4 it is relevant here to comment that assumptions which underlie commonly used expressions such as 'phrases', 'units', 'sections', 'beginning' and 'end' may not in fact be particularly appropriate in the consideration of all forms of dance. There are dances which extend through time to such an extent that it is their continuity that is crucial, not the fact that they have a beginning and ending of a particular character. Similarly it may be that a dance terminates in a certain place and time only to be picked up where it left off, at some later time, as though the interruption was unimportant.

Just as the link between analysing components and the form is made through acknowledging the existence of clusters of elements which occur simultaneously and which therefore may be perceived as related, so there is overlap between analysing the structure of a dance and interpreting it. This overlap occurs when certain movements or sections of the dance are identified as contributing most strongly to its character, as exhibiting qualities which are distinctive of the style and which act as indicators of its meaning(s).

In a brief discussion of Cunningham's *Sounddance*, Macaulay (1980) describes the formal characteristics that make this work distinctive – its urgency and drive are evident in the musical qualities in which power and time pulses reinforce the extremes of pace in the dancers' movement. The relationship between the design, i.e. the curtain flap, and the movement, produces the impact of an additional entry and exit which Cunningham himself controls. Croce (1977) pinpoints similar qualities although isolating the stark contrast of the quieter sections.

> *Sounddance* [the very title implies some musical response] is to a loud, fast-throbbing electronic score, *Toneburst*, by David Tudor: this conveys the same urgency and impulse as are to be found in the choreography. Through a flap in a low-hung curtain at the back, the dancers enter singly: they dance with vivid, fast, ecstatic commitment, but as if their moments of free expression are numbered; they return through the flap quickly one after another – Cunningham like a rear guard, the last to vanish.
>
> Macaulay (1980, p.735)

> In *Sounddance*, his backcloth [Mark Lancaster's] is a low-hanging drape with a vent from which the dancers emerge one by one to be swept into the rapids of the choreography; then they disappear into the vent... David Tudor's [score] for *Sounddance* sounds like an

53

excavation going on next door. In *Sounddance*, the sections
of non-stop allegro motion, the quieter sections of linked
poses, the fast editing interested me as much as they did
in the Events.

Croce (1977, p.202)

This vivid imagery encompasses in both cases the detail of the
components, and a formal, structural analysis contained in interpretative statements. In Macaulay's case this is through reference to
'estatic commitment, but as if their moments of free expression are
numbered' and in Croce, in the dancers being 'swept into the rapids
of the choreography'. Both statements are fully justified by reference
to the use of movement components and their structuring through
time. This reference to the observable features of the dance, the
components and the form, combined with allusive qualities and
poetic language, is often the substance of interpretative writing.

Four research examples
In order to demonstrate further the relevance of these general
principles of form, the four examples presented in Chapter 2 are
referred to again to show how components of the dance are incorporated into formal structures. The research examples are those by
Kaeppler (1971 and 1972) on Tongan Dance; Clifton and Hulme
(1978 and 1982) on step dancing in Norfolk; Hilton (1981) on the
dance of Court and Theatre 1690–1725 and Davis and Schmais
(1967) and Kagan (1978) on Doris Humphrey's work *Water Study*
(for full references see page 33).

A comparison of the structural patterns found by these authors is
laid out here. Table 2, from which this is derived, may be found on
pp. 57–59.

1. *The range of relationships between movement components is
distinctive in each dance style.*

Despite the restricted travelling pathways of step dancing, complexity of pattern occurs in the *juxtaposition of
numerous single step types*. These are based on 2, 3 and 5
beat rhythms and it is the relationship between the use of
the toe, ball of the foot and heel, in forward and backward directions, to particular metric divisions of beats
that creates step patterns in clearly punctuated rhythms.
In contrast, the distinctive relations in Tongan dance

54

occur between *parts of the upper body*, chiefly between the arm and hand surfaces, although the legs also take simple steps simultaneously and adjust the point of balance. Some dances, however, are performed in a sitting position. In the French Noble style the area of interest is found in *varied use of spatial elements*, in single steps, in floor pattern and in the placing of the dancers in the performing space combined with the shaping of gesture. Relation of dance emphasis to musical accentuation is important, both in *coinciding* with and *moving against* the phrasing. *Water Study* is also characterised by rhythmic relationships but in this case they are based on breathing and related to a quite different range of body shapes and dynamics. The same *movements* are performed with *varied strength and speed* and at *different times* in the dance.

2. *Images held in the moment, as on a photograph, reveal a style in relationship structures which is specific to each example*:

The crucial relationships in step dance structure are between the *emphasis within the step* and the *point in the musical structure* at which it occurs, since single, double and treble rhythms mark out the time design. *Minute differentiation* in the position of individual parts of the *lower arm and the hands* is characteristic of Tongan dance. Some of these positions would be recognisable as having specific meaning in a pictorial sense of depiction. It is the action of the *lower half* that varies by genre, hence an important element to note in relation to the *upper half* of the body. A typical position in the French Noble dance would produce the upright carriage with *arms either in parallel or opposition to the stepping leg*, with one dancer in positive relation to another, touching or making acknowledgement through inclination of head or body. In *Water Study* the rhythmic overlapping of phrasing results in individuals held at *different moments within similar patterns*, producing layers of arched designs.

3. *The ordering of phrases and sections of the dance through time results in recognisable patterning.*

Norfolk step dancing is ordered in *8-bar musical phrases*,

including a 2-bar finish, giving a clear and regular overall pattern, but the detailed unit of time is highly variable according to individual choice. Although Tongan dance is accompanied by song, it is the rigidly *fixed nature of sequences of body movement* which characterises the dance. Timing may not be as important as in other forms although it matters that the actual patterns of action are repeated exactly each time the dance is performed. The French Noble dance moves away from such spatially set forms in bodily design and into steps which *travel along linear and curved pre-ordained pathways*. Basic steps are combined in *different orders and quantities* in each dance to make longer phrases. The *musical and dance structures* are frequently *in parallel*, AABB or ABACA, although in repetitions the two may diverge. In rhythmic terms counter-emphasis may create different phrasing in the music from the dance. A sense of growing and shrinking, expanding and contracting, governs the time design of *Water Study*, both in individual movement and through the group. *Unison, canon and mirroring devices* are exploited to achieve this end.

4. *Although a dance may exhibit many kinds of relationship, some units, phrases and sections within the total web of relations are perceived to be more or less important.*

In the case of step dancing the more *complex* the unit or pattern, the greater is its significance. In Tongan dance the fixed structure decrees that certain movements are *by nature merely transitional* and others *crucial in conveying the sense of the dance*. Symmetrical figuration is a pronounced feature of the total structure of the dances of the French Noble period and, within this patterning, '*remarkable moments*' of emphasis are 'moved towards, reached and moved away from, in a ceaseless, rhythmic *ebb and flow*' (Hilton (1981, p.153). In *Water Study*, also, the structure makes a statement of symmetry in visual design, but there is *balance* within the total, between the *beginning* and the *end, with a climax* occurring in the middle. Hence the swelling and subsiding makes a crescendo to a specific moment then reverses its patterns to come to rest.

Table 2. Four research examples: the form of the dance

STEP DANCING: HULME, A-M, and CLIFTON, P, 1978
CLIFTON, P, and HULME, A-M, 1982

FORM OF THE DANCE

2.1 *Components related:*
steps placed after each other in time to make set patterns
'single' takes 2 beats; tap toe forward, step ball back
'double' takes 3 beats; tap toe forward, tap heel forward, step ball back OR tap toe forward, step ball back, heel drop
'treble' takes 5 beats; tap toe forward, tap heel forward, tap heel back, tap ball back, step toe

2.2 *At a point in time:*
tap patterns take place with dynamic emphasis in particular rhythms
'single' rhythm; 'and 1'
'double' rhythm; 'and a 1' OR '1 and a'
'treble' rhythm; 'and 1 and a 2'

2.3 *Through time:*
steps used to make sequences depending on individual's choice and to some extent on the music but within the 8-bar phrase divided into 6-bar step and 2-bar finish.
free phrasing within the structure arriving at the cadence points with the music, i.e. a non-repeating but rhythmic pattern
dancers join in and out at will

2.4 *High points with linear progression:*
rhythmic emphasis, speed and complexity of steps
provide climax points

2.5 *Total web of relations:*
the more difficult and complex the pattern the greater the importance of the pattern, relations are determined in performance, not in advance

TONGAN DANCE: KAEPPLER, A L, 1971
KAEPPLER, A L, 1972

FORM OF THE DANCE

2.1 *Components related:*
sitting and standing dances
6 groups of complex arm movements arising from combinations of single actions
direction linked with palm of hand
size of step and sitting position linked to sex and age of dancer

2.2 *At a point in time:*
same combinations of movements performed in different positions
multiplicity of combinations of basic patterns evident

2.3 *Through time:*
single movements repeated; different combinations of each movement with others
motifs, e.g. circling of hands round each other with palms facing forward, used alone, repeated, combined with other motifs

2.4 *High points with linear progression:*
points in the structure marked by sections, conventionalised beginnings, endings, movements known as 'transitional' ones are identifiable

2.5 *Total web of relations:*
total form clearly recognisable within the rules of the genre, e.g. set patterns containing groups of phrases whose importance is predetermined; greater importance placed on arm movements than on leg gestures.

Table 2 – *continued*

FRENCH NOBLE DANCE: HILTON, A L, 1981

FORM OF THE DANCE

2.1 *Components related:*
the same step could be performed in different directions, with an accent or without
a step unit (combination of 2–4 steps) usually used one measure of music with
emphasis on the first beat
movement without change of weight could also mark the first beat of the music

2.2 *At a point in time:*
arms may parallel leg action
arms may be in opposition to legs
arms elevated when feet are together
shoulder brought forward when arms are in opposition

2.3 *Through time:*
dancers move symmetrically making the same figure in opposite directions, or
same figure in same direction
combinations of circular and linear pathways combined with step patterns usually
starting with a straight line towards the presence then using side and centre spaces
to finish facing the presence
step patterns derived from combinations of step units
metric form of the music, i.e. AABB repeated or ABACA and the dance form may
echo or vary the emphasis in the music.

2.4 *High points with linear progression:*
movement towards a 'remarkable' point of emphasis, usually the strong beat of the
music and away from it in endless ebb and flow of rhythm
concordance or dissonance of dance and music emphases may produce highlights

2.5 *Total web of relations:*
total structure of each type of dance within the style is complex and recognisably
different from any other, patterns of structuring in general are common and tend
towards symmetical figuration

WATER STUDY By DORIS HUMPHREY:
Davis, M A, and SCHMAIS, C, 1967
KAGAN, E, 1978

FORM OF THE DANCE

2.1 *Components related:*
a single arc movement used by dancers at different levels and in various areas of the
space
a single movement performed with different, increasing dynamic emphasis

2.2 *At a point in time:*
overlapping of patterns so that at a moment different stages of each pattern are
evident
as above but some dancers with developed versions of the basic pattern
one individual may be moving or a small group or the total

2.3 *Through time:*
repeated successive movements
3 types of canon form, double lines of dancers mirror each other
parallel patterns
unison movement
variation in time within repeated phrases also enlarged with additional steps
enlarging and shrinking as individuals, small groups and the whole, using large
and small amounts of space

Table 2 – *continued*

2.4 *High points within linear progression:*
progression from quiet, low, rhythmic patterns to high-level excited ones, coinciding with increasingly more compact group design so that phrasing builds to
a climax point in the middle of the dance
sections clearly phrased with ebbing and flowing and 'swing' phrasing within movements

2.5 *Total web of relations:*
overall statement of symmetric structure of theme, swelling and subsiding taking in
static and then travelling patterns into crescendo
repetition of structure but in reverse order until movement comes to rest

© Adshead, J. adapted from authors' accounts.

CHAPTER 4

Interpreting the dance

by Pauline Hodgens

Interpretation
Concepts through which interpretations are made:
  Socio-cultural background
  Context
  Genre and style
  Subject matter
Concepts relating to the interpretation of a specific dance:
  Character
  Qualities
  Meanings/significances

Interpretation

Chapters 2 and 3 list and describe the range of possible ingredients out of which *any* dance may be created. Examples are given to show how *specific* genres, styles and *actual* dances vary because of the different selection and ordering of components. It is in relation to these perceptible features that dances can be discussed, described, analysed and notated.

There is, however, considerably more to understanding dance than having the ability merely to discern or notice its perceptible components and form(s). Understanding also encompasses meaning and value. In other words, the ability to interpret or make sense of particular perceptible features and the ability to evaluate what is perceived are also important in dance appreciation or analysis. This chapter focusses upon interpreting the dance and Chapter 5 upon evaluating the dance.

Interpreting is the term used to describe the process which brings out or demonstrates the meaning of a specific object, activity,

60

expression or form of behaviour. It may be thought of as 'translating', 'reading', 'accounting for', or 'making sense of' some object. The activity of interpreting generally exists in relation to those objects and events which are not wholly explained or understood with reference to their perceptible features alone. Many objects and events have a range and depth of meaning and significance the discovery of which demands close scrutiny and the specific act of 'translating' (or its equivalent). Thus interpreting combines the skills of *noticing, seeing* and *discerning* with those of *recognising, characterising* and *making sense of* the object or event in question. The process of interpreting includes the discerning of the features and form and the recognition of *character* and *qualities*. Interpreting is the process for discovering or revealing the *meaning* of certain objects or events.

Dances are examples of activities which can only be understood and appreciated through the process of interpretation. All dances have different features (components and forms) to be discerned and thus have different character and qualities to be recognised. The meaning and significance of each dance is realised through the process of discerning, recognising and characterising the objective and distinctive features. *An* interpretation of a dance (either a performance or a notated score) is an *account* which ascribes character, qualities and meanings to the features as they are discerned.

Dances vary considerably in both the context in which they appear (e.g. social, artistic, ritualistic) and the purposes which they serve (e.g. educational, therapeutic). Regardless of their setting and use, all dances are understood through the act of interpreting. Choreographers (makers of dances), performers and spectators all engage in the act of interpreting and, in one form or another, they all produce interpretations. The differences in their purposes means that their procedures and techniques are different and that the interpretations take a variety of forms. In relation to dance the concept of interpreting or interpretation is particularly complex and has to be considered in relation to the choreographer's, performer's and spectator's involvement in the dance.

The choreographer

In creating a dance the choreographer selects, manipulates, combines and structures specific components. They are treated in such a way that they exhibit the character, qualities and meanings pertinent to the choreographer's own purposes. The dance itself may be viewed as the rendering of an idea, a belief, a story (or a whole variety of other things) through the medium of movement. Whenever the choreographer has a degree of choice in the selection of the subject matter, certain freedom in the manipulation of the components and the opportunity to exercise imagination in the creation of dance, the process can be regarded as interpreting, and the dance as an interpretation.

The interpretative activity of the choreographer is constrained by a number of factors. Dances exist within a particular socio-cultural setting at a given time and place, they are performed by dancers, and they are appreciated by audiences (in those instances in which an audience is present during performance). These factors place limitations, which are more or less severe, upon the selection of content in terms of both the subject matter and the proposed treatment. For instance, Kaeppler (1971) records that in the dance celebrating the coronation of the King of Tonga in 1967 a choreographer used foot movements which he took from the dance of another genre. The ensuing discussions of what were seen to be inappropriate foot movements prohibited the audience from either appreciating his skill or enjoying the dance. Given that the selection is socially and culturally appropriate, the choreographer is limited to a greater or lesser extent by other considerations, including her/his own abilities and knowledge for creating with the movement material in relation to the selected content and treatment; the abilities of the dancers to execute whatever it is that is required, convincingly; and the abilities and knowledge of the audience to make sense of the ensuing dance.

The performer

When they dance, dancers also engage in interpretative activity, that is their performances (dances) are interpretations. Dances are prestructured in greater or lesser detail, although *some* may be improvised during performance or have improvised sections. In the *making* of the dance the choreographer may or may not allow the dancer to participate in the processes of selecting and manipulating the components, giving the dance character and qualities, and revealing the meanings. But, regardless of the nature or degree of the dancer's involvement at this stage, during performance the dancer interprets the dance. Just as the reader of a poem, through intonation and emphasis, can bring the words to life and give them *particular* qualities and meanings, so the dancer can affect the dance. Without changing the basic movement actions and the structures, the dancer can alter the qualities and meanings of the dance by attending to the subtleties of movement (e.g. the dynamics, the line, the placing of stress). Dancers give the dance shades of character, quality and meaning which are not necessarily prescribed by the choreography. In this sense the dancers interpret the roles as individuals and, according to their own technique, mastery and understanding, attempt to reveal the character, qualities and meanings of the dance as they see them. An interpretation understood in this sense is, therefore, a particular and distinctive performance by a dancer, dancers or a company.

In relation to different interpretations of, for example, the role of the bride in *Appalachian Spring*, Croce writes:

> Long ago when Graham was still dancing the part of the bride, I thought she had miscast herself, and when Ethel Winter and then Phyllis Gutelius took the role over, I felt sure of it ... Gutelius fills out her role with suggestions of things that are not explicit in the choreography. She's refined and vulnerable – a city bred girl, one feels, who has had servants, and the mother-to-be of children who will surely die. Nothing in her past has prepared her for the frontier except the necessity of making so hard a choice and the courage to see it through.
>
> Croce (1978, p.56)

Although this quotation refers to the dancers' interpretations of the role and therefore illustrates the point, it has to be borne in mind that it is also a critic's interpretation of the dancers' interpretation.

As in the case of Graham, Gutelius and Winter, dancers can become known for their interpretation of a role and some interpretations may be regarded as 'definitive'. For instance, *Le Spectre de la Rose* is forever associated with Nijinsky and *The Dying Swan* with Pavlova. Companies may also be known for their interpretations of certain dances; for instance, the Royal Ballet and Ballet Rambert are known for their own distinctive interpretations of *Dark Elegies* (see Chapter 8).

The spectator

The person who views the dance is also in the position of having to penetrate the meaning and significance. The spectator looks for the specific character, qualities and meanings with reference to both the structure and composition, and the performance, and, therefore, also engages in interpreting the dance. The subsequent account given by any member of the audience, whether it exists in an oral or written form (or even thought which could in principle be committed to words), is an interpretation of the dance.

Thus, in the case of dance, the concept of interpreting/ interpretation may be taken to mean:

— the choreographer rendering an idea by creating a dance with specific character, qualities and meanings: and/or

— the dancers revealing the meanings and significances of the dance through 'reading' the roles and giving them character and qualities in performance; and/or

— the spectators 'reading' the dance (structure and performance) and ascribing character, qualities and meanings and giving an explanatory account.

Whether interpretations are in the form of dances (performances or scores) or verbal accounts of dances, they are all directed towards the meaning and the significance of the dance. Movement accounts (dance performances) attempt to *display* the meaning and significance. The aim of verbal accounts is to *pinpoint* and *describe* the meaning and significance. In the latter case the spectator attends to the interrelations of the components, notes how they are presented and created within the extensive conventions and traditions of the dance, recognises and experiences the character and qualities produced, and thus penetrates the meaning of the dance. The ensuing account is in words. In the former case the choreographer selects, manipulates and displays the interrelated components and the dancer performs and presents them. Both, however, work through and within the relevant conventions and traditions to produce character and qualities and to make the meanings accessible. Their overall purpose is to engage the audience and/or the dancers in an understanding and an experience of the dance. The accounts of the choreographer and the dancer are in movement which is supported by the other components such as music, costume and lighting.

Having outlined the complex usage of the term 'interpretation' in the dance context and described the relevant skills, this chapter seeks to identify those concepts necessary for making a rational interpretation of the components and form of the dance in any of the modes just outlined. The concepts readily divide into two groups:

concepts through which interpretations are made and concepts relating to the interpretation of a specific dance.

Concepts through which interpretations are made (3.1)
Socio-cultural background (3.11)
Context (3.12)
Genre and style (3.13)
Subject matter (3.14)
Concepts relating to the interpretation of a specific dance (3.2)
Character (3.21)
Qualities (3.22)
Meanings/significance (3.23)

Concepts through which interpretations are made (3.1)

Dances are social and cultural products which embody, and are created and received in relation to, the conventions and traditions of a particular time and place. The understanding of a dance, therefore, relies upon knowledge of that time and place. Knowledge, deriving from four sources which themselves are interrelated in an exceedingly complex way, allows access to the meaning and significance of the dance in question. The sources are the socio-cultural background, the context, the genre and style and the subject matter of the dance.

Socio-cultural background (3.11)

All dances are found within a social and cultural setting and relate directly to the general beliefs and values of that time and place. Their creation and reception is according to the traditions and conventions as they exist for the particular group of people. Much of the knowledge which is required for understanding is simply that which is accrued by living within the society in question. One of the major factors to be taken into account in relation to the interpretation of any dance is the range and type of human movement, expression and communication used by the people from whom the particular dance emerges, for this determines, in part, the meaning of the dance. The materials of the dance are not neutral, they carry meanings or significances which are independent of the dance situation. The basic movement material of the dance is impregnated with meanings with which the choreographer, performers and audience have to come to terms.

There is widespread opinion that movement used in dance is based directly upon the movement of everyday life and that, therefore, knowledge of this is crucial to understanding, especially when considering works from another culture. For example, Bartenieff's system of 'choreometrics' is designed to describe movement style in dance and, according to Gellerman (1978), tests the hypothesis that dance 'as a form of behaviour is an organised elaboration, repetition and intensification of everyday movement patterns' (p.124). Kaeppler (1972) also assumes that there are 'elements selected from all possible human movements and positions and are recognized as significant by people of a given dance tradition' (p.174). In the case of Tongan dance her researches reveal that some movements are 'stylizations of everyday and ceremonial life' (p.194). Walther (1979) argues that gesture is the 'universal element' in dance but that it is 'culture bound'. She suggests that

> all stylistic differences in dance are a result of, and can be accounted for in relation to differences in gestural language i.e. the particular gestural communication within a culture.

> Walther (1979, p.69)

It is the 'profound symbolic meaning of cultural systems of gesture' which brings dance styles into being and, therefore, the dance style represents a 'whole gestalt of emotional and psychological states of human behaviour within a cultural setting'. The problem lies in coming to understand the gestural basis and, therefore, what is being communicated.

In an attempt to understand how movement choices are embedded in the socio-religious philosophy of the people, Gellerman (1978) undertook a study of Hasidic dance patterns. Her study is a microcosm of this larger concern since its focus is a simple pattern consisting of four steps and the relationship of this pattern to three very specific contexts. Nonetheless it illustrates the complexity of interpretation even when the parameters are clearly known. She examines the 'mayim' dance pattern as it appears in three American Hasidic communities in New York. The performance of the 'mayim' is analysed through a comparison of the three groups. She locates common characteristics of all Hasidic dance patterns then distinct differences between the three communities in their performance of these patterns.

Hasidism is an Eastern European branch of Orthodox Judaism which began in the late eighteenth century, and which stresses mystical experience and ecstasy in song and movement rather than the Talmud-based style of worship. It caused a revival of music, song and dance in association with social and religious occasions.

According to Gellerman the three communities respectively represent conservative, moderate and progressive attitudes within the shared codes of Hasidism. The differences derive from the personality of the head of each group and from their regional origins respectively in Hungary, South-West Poland and White Russia. She isolates differences in attitudes to dress; to the roles of the sexes; to modern technology; to emotionalism in worship; to western values; and to the use of the English language.

The dances, she demonstrates, contain movements from Eastern European, American and Israeli cultures but they are performed in a 'distinctively Hasidic style' (p.120). She suggests that common values shape the use of movement, wherever it has originated. Since men and women dance separately, two repertoires have developed, the one very active in style, the other more modest. Some dances, notably the Eastern European ones, are performed by both sexes while others are danced by men or women. Technical virtuosity plays a large part in men's solo improvisations while women's 'Hasidic Charlestons' reveal American influences.

The 'mayim' dance was created in the 1940s in Israel and has spread to many parts of the world. It has a characteristic 'grape vine' step where the right foot crosses in front of and then behind the left as a closed circular group of women travels to the left. The shared characteristics in performance relate to body postures, stance and use of effort elements in a way that can be seen to link with everyday movement and dress. The differences are located in the degree of communication between participants; subtle alterations in body shape; the range of spatial pattern; the use of the weight factor; rhythm and flow. She argues that these choices reflect the ideological differences between groups and concludes that

> embedded in the plain, unadorned performance of the mayim pattern are the Hasidic ideals of discipline, simplicity and humility.
>
> Gellerman (1978, pp.129–30)

Other socio-cultural knowledge relevant to the understanding of dance is described in further detail in the following sections on the remaining three sources. This is done with reference to appropriate examples and, in particular, in relation to the four research examples already cited in Chapters 2 and 3.

Context (3.12)

Each society and culture may have many types of dancing, each of which may be used for specific purposes. In the United Kingdom in the latter half of the twentieth century dance appears, for instance, in the contexts of artistic/theatrical, social and religious life and may be used for purposes such as entertainment, celebration, worship, therapy, socialisation and education. The context determines, in large measure, appropriate and inappropriate types and methods of interpretation. For instance, within the context of art in Western society, interpretations of dances are guided and bounded by art practices and theory. One of the prevalent views of art is, for example, that each art form works with and solves problems created by a particular medium and its materials. It involves a craft and technique which is developed within conventions and traditions, the most specific of which are genres and styles. The art work is produced, exists and is appreciated simply for what it is, for its own sake and for its individual meaning. Dance as art, therefore, has to be approached, understood and appreciated within these parameters.

This view of art, however, may coexist with others. The notions of what constitutes art and art works, of what art can do or say, of the kinds of subject matter and ranges of treatment that are appropriate, fluctuate according to a number of factors. Because of, for instance, the social and cultural mixture of peoples within any Western country there are a variety of practices and understandings related to art as well as constant adaptation. These general factors produce different, and even unique, beliefs and conventions about art in general and forms and styles in particular. In turn they influence dance as it exists within that context. Thus, particular content, techniques and standards for both the choreography and performance are associated with specific peoples of a given time and place. This creates certain expectations and values for the appreciation of dance.

Dance is similarly context-bound when found as an aspect of religion, ritual or social life. The contextual considerations are as complex as those of art. They include the same kind of extensive range of historical, social and cultural factors. Amongst any given group of people there may be forms of religious, ritual and social dance, each associated with certain beliefs and particular systems. Within each form there may be groups of dances that display features which are alike enough to group them and call them genres and styles. Each of these will prescribe certain conventions for the production, performance and the reception of the dance.

For instance, evidence for the existence of dance in the ritual of the Christian church abounds (for a comprehensive account see Backman 1952), although analysing the exact nature of the various forms is difficult. There is no doubt that the performance of dances played an important part in the ritual of the church until the 1800s. Backman quotes detailed accounts of many types of dance associated with death, and with a wide range of perceived functions:

types: night wakes
      burial dances
      dances around the coffin
      memorial dances
      dances in churchyards
      dances of the dead
      dances of the angels

functions: to protect the living from the dead
      to comfort the dead
      to rejoice in the resurrection
      to protect the dead from demons
      to celebrate a child's unity with the angels
      the dead, dancing as skeletons, draw others to their death.

Some of these examples may be allegorical rather than actual, the interpretations of their significance are many. However, they can be grouped round the central tenets of the Christian faith, for example the triumph over death through the resurrection; the power of evil derived from the devil; and the capacity of death to equalise all members of a society. Some forms hark back to earlier mystical and pre-Christian beliefs.

Dances within each context have specific purposes which could be outlined in a similar way. Together, the context and purposes prescribe or influence the craft and content of creation, re-creation and performance of the relevant dance and the nature of any spectatorial involvement. Thus, there may be distinctive techniques, standards and expectations for choreography (where it exists and can be identified), performance and appreciation (in those cases where it is appropriate). There are, of course, many examples of dance which, although they exist in one context, rely upon another for an adequate interpretation. There are, for instance, examples of dances in the context of art which are social or ritualistic in origin and examples of social forms of dance which are religious in origin. In many instances it is even difficult to say with certainty what the context might be. The distinctions between social, ritual, religious or artistic dance are often blurred.

In some instances the choreographers take the dance and its associated imagery from one context, e.g. that of the ritual of the church, and use it in another situation, e.g. that of making art. The rich history of dance practice within church ritual, coupled with the literature of Christianity as embodied in the Old Testament, has provided the substance of many artistic dance forms.

As Manor (1980) points out, biblical events have become the historical and mythological heritage that people carry with them just as Greek legends, too, are part of this tapestry. Although the narratives may have little to do with current religious beliefs, or those of the choreographer, they serve to convey a moral message. The characters are richly drawn, the dramatic value of the stories is intense. It is the mixture of poetry, chronicles of events, allegories and fiction that produces this portrait of mankind. The meanings it offers are many, most stories can be interpreted in simple or complex terms. The multi-layered character of the Bible has fascinated the Western world for generations. It is hardly surprising that the material should be explored in a variety of art forms and reinterpreted time after time.

The practice of using essentially religious material in making a ballet or dance has been prevalent throughout the existence of the art form of dance. The Jesuits of the sixteenth century, for example, staged *Goliath* and *Joseph* in honour of contemporary events and as educational tools. In recent years Cohan has taken the theme of Jacob and Esau in his work *Hunter of Angels* (1967).

When protagonists of the religion perform the dances themselves, then presumably there is still a link with religious practice as the dance serves both as an art and as a religious expression. Some twentieth-century groups of dancers perform in religious settings too, whether as community groups performing simple symbolic movement patterns, or as semi-professional or professional dancers performing highly structured art works based on religious themes.

In the theatre of the twentieth century biblical themes continue to occur. For example, Manor (1980) lists many versions of the Salome story and a selection from the choreographers using this theme includes:

1894 Fuller
1907 Allan
1908 Rubinstein
1946 Lifar
1948 Ruth St Denis
1970 Béjart

and, perhaps amounting to an obsession, Lester Horton's six versions made between 1931 and 1950. Lindsay Kemp's later adaptation of Oscar Wilde's account was one of the most controversial.

Coincidentally both de Valois and Shawn produced versions of *Job* in 1931. The former version, which used Blake's paintings as an inspiration and the music of Vaughan Williams, was the basis for a later television choreography by Cohan, *The Story of Job*, in 1975.

The Prodigal Son, similarly, has provided a source for many choreographers over a range of styles. In 1812 Gardel created an opera ballet for the Paris Opera, while in this century Balanchine, in 1929, Jooss, in 1931, and Lichine, in 1938, all produced Prodigal Sons.

Graham, among other modern dance choreographers, has used female characters from the Bible as heroine figures, for example in the solo of *Judith* of 1950, which became the *Legend of Judith* in 1962. She also took a sect of flagellants as the basis for the dance *El Penitente* in 1940.

Limon's *There is a Time* (1956) takes as its philosophy, a view of the order and rightness of events, and transforms this into a dance. Even the creation of the world itself has been the subject matter of dance, albeit full-length evening works of approximately three hours.

Although the broad consideration of the socio-cultural background is crucial to the understanding of the dance, the identification of the particular context and purpose points to those facets which are of direct and immediate concern. If more detailed information is required about the relevant knowledge for understanding, then attention has to be given to categories of dance which exist within specific contexts, that is to those categories known as genres.

Genre and style (3.13)

In relation to the broad categories of both socio-cultural background and context, dances fall into groups known as genres and styles. The history of dance as a Western theatre art, for example, reveals a number of changes, developments, innovations and even personalities which mark certain points in, or periods of, time, and a number of groups, companies or schools which show a divergence or consensus in practice. This overall process of polarisation and categorisation reveals groups of dances which are different although very often closely related. Thus, different types of theatre dance such as ballet, modern dance and stage dance can be classified as different genres.

Genres are groups of dances the individual members of which have enough in common to make them collectively distinctive. The distinctiveness of each genre can be seen in the marked similarities in the selection of the components of the constituent dances and in types of structure and patterning. The *reasons* for the differences between the genres, however, are to be found not in the components of the dances but in the beliefs and values associated with the form of life of the society and culture in which the dance is found (that is, in the context of art, religion, social life etc.). Genres are 'crystallisations' of specific knowledge, beliefs, ideas, techniques, preferences or values around which particular traditions and conventions for producing and receiving dance have grown. In the case of Tongan dance there are six identifiable genres, three of which are 'living' and three of which are traditional. Two of the genres have as their focus 'creating beauty' and the other four are more directly concerned with interpreting poetry. All Tongan dance is 'performance requiring skill in which the hands are rhythmically moved while singing' (Kaeppler 1971, p.176). The four interpretative genres provide a visual accompaniment to the poetry while the genres concerned with creating beauty focus upon the execution of the dance motifs. Different genres are used according to the occasion.

Within this broad categorisation of genre it is possible to draw distinctions between constituent groups and identify them as particular styles. For instance, ballet may be pre-romantic, romantic, classical or modern in style and these may be referred to as *general styles*. Within the same genre and general style there may be more specific styles which relate to, for example, the country or region of origin, or the individuals, family, community or company by whom they are performed. For instance, classical ballet (a general style) is significantly different from country to country. Even companies within one country may exhibit characteristic differences.

Clifton and Hulme (1982) discuss the genre and general style known as traditional step dancing as it is found in North Norfolk, that is from the area covering 'Cromer in the east to Wells-next-the-Sea in the west (some twenty miles)' and extending 'inland ten miles to Aylsham and Fakenham' (p.29). Within 'pure' step dancing of the area (that is excluding dances which merely contain 'stepping') there are three specific styles: Norfolk stepping which is intrinsic to the area and deeply rooted; the older Traveller's stepping derived from gypsies and other travellers; and Lancashire stepping. Within each of these categories there are specific and distinctive individual or family styles. All differences in style lie in the rhythms and phrases, the presence or absence of heel beats, the music, or the shoes which are worn.

These stylistic differences can be discerned in the dances for they are the result of the components having been selected and related in a characteristic way. They are accounted for in relation to a number of factors. For instance, Percival writes in relation to the style of the Royal Ballet:

> Ashton has created more than ballets. The dancers who grew up dancing his works developed in the way he led them ... Consequently Ashton's ballets have been the biggest single influence on the way the Royal Ballet dances. What is sometimes called the 'English style' with its poise, its purity, its freshness, is really the Ashton style.
>
> Royal Opera House Covent Garden programme notes
> (19 March 1982)

This description points not only to the important notions of choreographic style and performance style but also demonstrates the interrelatedness of all the stylistic categories in dances exhibiting distinctive sets of characteristics.

Choreographers have their own inimitable style (albeit one that may change and develop through time). The style is recognised as a characteristic procedure which makes an important, identifiable and distinctive contribution to the genre and general style within which it is found (as in the case of Ashton). A large number of *choreographic styles* can generally be identified within general styles and genres. In the case of the French dance of the court and theatre as found during the reign of Louis XIV, 1700–35, there are within the Noble style a number of specific styles and types. Some of these pertain to the 'character' with whom the dance is concerned but others are examples of the distinctive choreographic styles, of Feuillet, Rameau and Tomlinson, for example.

Individual dancers have a unique style as a result of their personal movement characteristics and their physical, technical, and performance abilities. Many dancers are recognised as having their own *performance style* as distinct from, but in relation to, the styles already mentioned. This is also the case with regard to companies. They, too, have what can be identified as a particular performance style.

Any comprehensive analysis of the style of a single dance (or a group of dances) would have to take into account all of these factors which make it both distinctive and one of a type. The grounds for recognising or determining style are found in the perceptible features of the dance, that is, in the various components which are selected and the relationships which are created.

With reference to the components (particular movements, lights, set etc.) and to their interrelations (motifs, phrases etc), it is possible to identify and account for the genre in which the dance is located, the general style to which it belongs and the specific choreographic and performance styles which are exhibited. For instance, *Water Study* is an example of the genre of modern dance: its general style is early twentieth century American and it is one of the first of this genre and style to be performed without music, using a group of dancers in a non-metrical way. The dance also has European affinities, related to the work of Wigman in particular, and some stylistic features, therefore, must be traceable to this source. Humphrey's own choreographic style is recognisable within the dance especially in the use of fall and recovery and the non-literal nature of expression. The performance style of the company and individuals involved will also be important in any analysis. There will, for example, be distinctive differences between the dance as performed by the women dancers trained by Humphrey and the dancers in the all-male African version. Using the tools of Labananalysis and Effort/shape, Davis and Schmais (1967) identify stylistic elements of

Water Study and on this *basis* reveal its 'distinctive style'. On the *basis* of the movement content, Kagan (1978) compares the style of *Water Study* with that of Taylor's *Three Epitaphs*.

In summary, genres and styles are characteristic selections and orderings of the basic components of the dance guided by certain conventions and traditions derived from social and cultural life. Those things which have meaning, significance and value for a given society and culture at a particular time, and for a choreographer and performers, are, in some measure, captured and preserved by selected and specific dance patterns and forms known as genres and styles.

Genres and styles have such distinctive characteristics that many individual dances may be easily and accurately identified and categorised. Where there are adequate records (descriptions and scores) it is possible to reconstruct in the styles of certain periods and people despite authenticity problems created by the time/social/cultural gap. Within genres and styles, however, there is considerable freedom and fluidity. Their specific conventions and traditions are general enough to allow for the creation of dances which are individual and, in their overall effect and meaning, unique. They also demonstrate a gradual evolution or development under the influences of changes in the culture and changing choreographers and performers.

Thus genres and styles provide traditions and conventions in relation to which, and through which, dances can be created, performed and appreciated. Under the practical and ideological constraints and freedoms of the genre and style a choreographer selects, manipulates, relates and displays certain components. The individuality of the dance is demonstrated in its choreographic, performance and aesthetic effects but it is, at the same time, firmly embedded in specific conventions and traditions. In the same way the dancer's freedom is constrained by and rooted in the stylistic requirements of both the genre and the choreographer. In turn the spectator's freedom to interpret and appreciate is both created and constrained by the traditions and conventions of the genre and style.

The successful creation, performance, understanding and appreciation of any dance are dependent upon a thorough knowledge of how the relevant genre and style 'works' both practically and ideologically. Anyone in Western society would recognise ballet, but without knowing how the genre and specific style determine the structure and presentation, and how and why the dance in question can be seen to have meaning and worth, the understanding and appreciation of the dance in that form would be limited.

Changes in style and the recognition of new genres often come about simply because existent genres and styles are not capable of expressing or handling a new or different range of ideas. Where there is a new range of possibility there often has to be a new means of expression. Thus the history of dance records changes in style and the gradual formulation of new genres which exist as both continuations of and reactions to what has gone before.

At the present time programmes of dance (as art) in the large cities of the Western world would offer works within different genres and ranging over a number of styles. Although each style can be seen to be the product of its age, in the sense that it could only have emerged at that time, works from that era, and new works using the same range of movement technique and expressive characteristics, continue to be performed. The 'classics' then, and some fundamental features of the style, transcend the constraints and conventions of the period in which they were made.

In the last two hundred years the gradual evolution of the art form of dance has produced many overlapping styles. Just as some aspects of Humphrey's work have strong links with classical ballet, others, such as her focus on movement for its own sake, link her with Cunningham and later modern dancers. In *Water Study* she was already laying the foundation for a new aesthetic of time for modern dance based on movement patterns alone rather than on music. This notion, almost unknown in classical ballet, is now common in dance as art.

Taken many stages further, Cunningham rejects story-type meanings and changes his use of time and space. The dancers he uses may have several different trainings rather than a single classical or modern technique but they are, nevertheless, highly skilled. Some choreographers who have emerged from Cunningham's company or school have chosen to change the movement vocabularly and to use untrained dancers doing 'ordinary' movement, standing, walking, sitting etc. Any historian will see the significant links – Isadora Duncan, among others, was concerned with natural, unsophisticated, 'sincere' movement, uncluttered by artificial techniques.

It seems as though the life of a society gives rise to a dance form which matches its social, intellectual and artistic preoccupations.

The form may take on a life of its own, however, and push on to the logical artistic limits of that kind of expression. The court dances, for example, became theatricalised with the increasingly ritualised structure of court life and eventually took to the stage to be performed by specialists. In so doing, some works were created which stand as prime exemplars of the style and which embody the artistic strengths of that mode of expression, to be handed on to the next generation.

A parallel can be made in the development of modern dance – certain works stand out such as Ruth St Denis' *Radha* (1906), Isadora Duncan's *La Marseillaise* (*c*.1914), Martha Graham's *Lamentation* (1930), Merce Cunningham's *Rainforest* (1968), Yvonne Rainer's *Trio A* (1966 and later versions) and Trisha Brown's *Accumulation Pieces* (1971).

In London in the autumn of 1983 one could have seen works by classical choreographers ranging from Taglioni, through Petipa to Ashton and Corder; by modern dance choreographers from Cohan through Davies and Bruce to Alston; and 'new' dance choreographers from Fulkerson through Clark to Booth. Each style speaks in its own way of the diversity and richness of forms of dance and their expressive potential.

Subject matter (3.14)

In very general terms all dances are 'about', 'related to' or 'concerned with' something. It is the 'something' which is the subject matter. In a limited sense the subject matter of any dance can be described and discussed independently, just as theatre programme notes, for instance, relate the story of a ballet or the idea behind a dance. There is, however, an important sense in which the subject matter of the dance cannot be considered apart from the dance itself. Although the dance may be based upon, for example, a straightforward story, the detailed nature of what is conveyed by the dance is peculiar to the dance itself. The *precise* statement and the *particular* meaning are discovered by a consideration of the detail of both the subject matter as it is selected for the dance and the way it is treated within the dance. Dances are particulars and are created by the selection of *this* movement and *this* incident, treated in *this* way, in the service of *this* end. It is the *selection* of the components and the *treatment* of the selection which creates points of special interest and which, for example, stresses, enhances, exaggerates, highlights,

77

blurs or restates specific aspects and in so doing gives rise to a unique statement. Dances are thus interpreted in the light of what can be reasonably understood to be the content of the work as it is both created and affected by the types of treatment which are employed. The layers of meaning associated with many dances, and especially those found in the context of art, are created and appreciated through the subtle interplay of content and treatment.

Out of all the possible types and ranges of statements which could be made about water and the sea in the form of dance, Humphrey's *Water Study* creates only one. The dance relates to the subject matter of water in a very specific and limited way, and both the components and the treatment are selected to this end. Siegel writes of the dance:

> it is not specifically symbolic; that is, you cannot say one dancer represents the wave and another the spray, or even that one part of the stage is the shore and another the ocean. Each dancer contains within herself all the elements of all the images, so that she is creating simultaneously the ebb and flow of energy, the evolving design of an expanding and shrinking body shape, and a changing stage landscape as she travels through the space.
>
> Siegel (1979, p.29)

Davis and Schmais (1967) show how the mood, atmosphere and meaning of the dance spring from the types of movements which Humphrey selected and her specific way of treating them. Through the treatment of selected movements a dance is created which brings into being specific dynamic and spatial images of water.

Considerations of the subject matter and treatment of a dance are closely bound up with the concepts of genre and style. Selections of material and ways of structuring, manipulating and presenting them are constrained by the conventions and traditions of the genre, general style, and choreographic and performance styles. As already noted in the previous section, genres and styles relate directly to the beliefs, ideas, life-styles and values within a given society and culture (in some instances they may even relate to myths, historic events and personages). This being the case, they specify (albeit in some instances very generally) and anticipate the ends, aims, purposes and outcomes of the associated dances.

To a great extent, therefore, genres and styles place constraints upon, and in some cases actually specify, the nature and range of the material of the dance and the relevant kinds of techniques for creating, performing and presenting it. Within these conventions and traditions there is a certain and variable amount of freedom for the choreographer and performer.

Dances which have historic precedent are remembered in general outline, or varying degrees of detail, by the group or community which dances them. In these cases the content and the treatment is known. They are simply repeated at the appropriate time or a new version is created. In the case of dances which have no historic precedent the apparent 'newness' is limited in as much as it is restricted by a web of constraints created by the conventions and traditions of the genre and style within which it can be located. In the case of, for instance, Tongan dances, the 'living' genres are very closely related to the traditional genres in terms of both content and treatment.

The subject matter of Tongan dance is made explicit by the narrative of the poetry. The treatment of the narrative is, however, abstruse. References to people and deeds are made in roundabout ways or through symbols. For instance, the lines (as recorded by Kaeppler 1972)

> Kulukona flower of the tropic bird created
> Plucked by the warm breeze
> Who is surprised at his fragrance . . .

refer to Tungi (kulukona flower), who was born (created) the highest male chief in the land (the tropic bird). Tonga (the warm breeze) has picked Tungi for her next King. None is surprised by his greatness (fragrance) because he is the kulukona flower and of great parentage. Allusion of this kind is the essence of Tongan poetry. In the accompanying dance the movements are not realistic but are equally as abstruse. Thus, Tongan dance can only be understood when the treatment of double abstraction is appreciated.

Some of the French Noble style dances have an obvious subject matter in the form of a mythological or heroic plot. They were created as lavish spectacles but the treatment was designed to both reflect and formalise the established patterns of the prevalent social hierarchy.

Step dancing has no obvious external subject matter. Its 'content' lies in the step patterns which are then grouped according to the structural conventions of the style. The two Tongan dance genres which aim to create 'beauty' similarly have no subject matter. The dance is accompanied by two lines of poetry which are repeated but, as the aim is to produce a good performance of the motifs, the concern is with the movement content and not the poetic allusion. In the case of the dance of the French Noble style there are examples of social dances in which the content is basically stepping and gesturing. They are treated, however, to convey the ideal qualities such as 'nobility', 'serenity', 'grace' and 'wit'.

The Tongan example shows the difficulties (even impossibilities) or interpreting a dance of another society, culture or time. The difficulties exist simply because the means of understanding are not available to 'outsiders' unless they have considerable knowledge and experience of the relevant cultural and social factors. But even the interpretation and understanding of dances within one's own culture when they have no precedent (new forms and types) is equally difficult. In these cases the known conventions and traditions of genres and styles are not applicable except in indicating what the dance is *not*. Any interpretation relies upon noting what is present (and absent) in the dance and also upon the kind of treatment it is given. In the absence of the guidelines of genre and style the only other factor to which the percipient may have recourse would be to the aims and purposes of the creator of the dance.

In summary, the concepts which have been identified as those through which interpretations are made are those pertaining to the socio-cultural background of the dance, the context in which the dance is found, the genre to which the dance belongs and the subject matter with which the dance deals.

Concepts relating to the interpretation of a specific dance (3.2)

The knowledge outlined in the previous section forms the relevant background information through which dances can be understood and appreciated. It is this knowledge which allows the percipient to ascribe *character*, *qualities* and *meanings* or *significance* to the perceptible components and forms of the dance. The notions of character, quality and meaning/significance, as they are used in the context of the interpretation of dance, are inextricably related. They are discussed separately here simply because each one points to and elucidates a slightly different facet of an interpretation.

Character (3.21)

The character of each dance can be described with reference firstly, to the type to which it belongs and its choreographer; that is, the overall location in time and place. Secondly, it can be described with reference to the subject matter selected and treatment employed. A dance may said to be of an identifiable genre, within a specific style, and to have a certain subject matter which is treated in a particular way.

Qualities (3.22)

Interpretative activity concerned with attributing qualities to the dance is directed towards the unique and particular achievements of the performance in terms of the effects, impressions, appearances, moods and atmospheres which it creates (these are collectively referred to as qualities). Unique qualities can be attributed to a dance in each and every performance. These are generally described as aesthetic qualities and the experience of them as aesthetic experience.

The concept of the aesthetic (and its cognates) is philosophically complex and is, therefore, frequently and hotly debated. In this chapter it is assumed that, broadly speaking, aesthetics is concerned with those problems and issues which pertain to a distinctive kind of interest in, approach to, appreciation and appraisal of, any 'object' (in this case dance). It is assumed that an aesthetic interest in the dance is an interest which focusses upon it 'for its own sake'. This being the case the percipient may be involved with both:

— discerning and understanding the features of the dance as they are perceived (literally and imaginatively) through the appropriate concepts of the relevant conventions and traditions; and
— recognising the appearances, effects, moods or atmospheres and her or his own impressions or experiences of the dance.

This aspect of interpretation does not and cannot stand in isolation from the other aspects. Aesthetic qualities are not divorced from the character of the dance nor from its meaning. Appearances, effects, impressions, moods and atmospheres as well as the character of the dance are created by the treatment of the subject matter within the conventions and traditions of the genre and style.

Different genres and styles value and produce specific types of qualities. Kaeppler writes that 'each society has standards for the production and performance of cultural forms' and that they constitute an aesthetic for that society. An individual cannot be said to properly understand the aesthetic principles of an alien culture unless he can anticipate indigenous evaluations of artistic performances or products.

Kaeppler (1971, p.175)

The aesthetic notions and values pertaining to the dance of various societies and cultures are thus embedded within their concepts of genre and style. Walther remarks that all of the elements which form the basis of all dance are

stylized very differently in the dance of each culture, according to a diversity of cultural values, aesthetic concepts and individual creativity.

Walther (1979, p.68)

The notion of 'aesthetic quality' (conceived of in the way just described) has two strands. It may refer to what are most conveniently called the qualities of the object or to the qualities of the percipient's experience of the object. A dance has certain perceptible and verifiable components and form(s). When these are perceived in the light of the interest described, the dance has certain appearances, that is it looks, sounds or appears in certain ways or as certain things. The appearances, and conjunctions of appearances, create certain perceptible effects, results, combinations, consequences, upshots or outcomes, some of which are moods and atmospheres. All of these taken together may create impressions and moods within the spectator. Aesthetic descriptions may thus apply to the qualities which can be attributed to the dance or to the percipient's responses to the dance. In all cases the descriptions are based upon the perceptible features of the dance even although they may be accounts of how they strike the percipient in terms of character and qualities. For instance, Kagan (1978) writes of Taylor's *Three Epitaphs* that a 'predominant expressive element is created through the device of both body shape and an effort body attitude' (p.77). In a description which is predominantly aesthetic she says that the dance 'evokes images of defensiveness and defeat' and that they are maintained so 'consistently as to exaggerate the level of absurdity, so that we are amused as much as we are disturbed'. She accounts for the description of the dance and her own responses and statements by referring to a 'constellation of factors', that is the 'slumped, closed body attitude, split upper/lower, small kinesphere, and in-ward rotation' (p.79).

Each genre and style has, to some degree, its own 'aesthetic'. Specific qualities are valued and all examples of dances within its domain exhibit these 'quality' characteristics. They can be antici-pated and discussed prior to and apart from any score or perform-ance of the dance. The percipient is prompted to look for specific qualities by virtue of the fact that the dance is an example of a certain genre and style. Within this broad aesthetic, however, each and every dance necessarily creates its own unique qualitative structure and although it stands in relation to the general 'aesthetic' it is unique. Every individual dance on each occasion of performance involves the percipient in a different and distinctive experience and thus the qualities attributed to the dance may vary. Familiarity with the dance, however, especially in those cases in which the meaning is found on a variety of levels, brings a deeper understanding and with it the awareness of a greater range of qualities or different qualities altogether.

The aesthetics of step dancing relate to how the steps are per-formed and to the nature and complexity of the phrasing and rhythm. These are appreciated in terms of the liveliness, vigour and fun of the dance. In the same way the aesthetics of the French Noble style relate to how the steps and gestures are performed and the ability to produce qualities which are 'noble', 'lively', 'graceful' and 'elegant'.

Kaeppler (1971) lays out the aesthetics of Tongan dance. Two concepts are important in this context, those of 'mālie' and 'māfana'. The dance has to be 'well done' (mālie) in terms of the 'craftsman-ship of the composition', 'the appropriateness of the selections' and the skill of the performer. The beauty of the performance is particu-larly important and it is seen in terms of gracefulness, softness and the use of the head. The dance also has to produce 'inward warmth and exhilaration' (māfana) for both the spectator and the performer.

Although the dances of Humphrey may have a general aesthetic, the aesthetic qualities of *Water Study* spring from the effects, moods and atmosphere which the individual dance creates. Davis and Schmais (1967) refer to the 'images it seems to create' and Siegel (1979) describes the dance as a 'collection of images of water'. These, she suggests, are created by the silence and the fourteen dancers who 'both collectively and individually' use movements that 'correspond to its energies and spatial configurations' (p.29). The dancers and their movements make the 'watcher's eye travel across the stage following the movement like a current or wave' and make the viewer experience certain things as, for instance, the 'emptiness to the left as a vast expanse' (p.30).

Qualities which are ascribed to the dance may have a variety of sources. Individual components may set up a certain kind of appearance, mood or impression; for example, the movement of the dancers, the light as it strikes the set, or the music may be the *source* of specific qualities. Any of these alone, or in any combination, may create noticeable qualities. In the same way, motifs or phrases within the dance may give rise to qualitative ascriptions. Aesthetic ascriptions may, therefore, be concerned with qualities of the whole dance or qualities of aspects of the dance; they may exist as major interpretative statements or aspects of interpretative statements.

Meanings/significance (3.23)

Interpreting the dance has so far been described as the recognition and attribution of character and qualities. The overall aim of interpreting is, however, the understanding and appreciation of its meanings and/or significance. In most cases the meanings and significances are nothing other than the character and qualities of the dance. Each dance is a unique treatment of certain subject matter by a choreographer and/or performers within specific and identifiable conventions and traditions. Each dance, therefore, has a distinctive character and creates unique qualities. The understanding of the point or purpose of the dance depends upon the individual's knowledge and abilities to recognise these and relate to them. The meaning of Tongan dance, for instance, is tied to the occasion and thus to the history and culture of the people. Furthermore it can only be appreciated if the principle of double abstraction is known and understood. It is the ability to interpret both the poetry, and the movement as it relates to the poetry, which reveals the meaning of the dance. Dance of the French Noble style has meaning and significance in relation to either the subject matter of the extravaganza or the acting out of the social interaction, or to the statements about the social status of different groups as shown through the exhibition of manners and politeness.

In contrast, step dancing has no 'meaning'. Its significance lies in the fact that it is a social activity of a specific type and quality and that it is used on certain occasions such as harvest frolics, family parties, and gatherings at the local public house. On some occasions the dances are competitive.

The artistic statement or meaning of *Water Study* lies in the nature of what is 'said' or 'displayed' or 'read' about the subject matter – water. As an artist's image of water its significance lies in the precise and unique nature of the statement. Davis and Schmais suggest that it creates images of

> low calm swells . . . increasing in size and turbulence . . . to clashing currents . . . massive breaking waves . . . long rushes of currents . . . lighter cascades . . . gentle laps of water wash up against the beach.
>
> Davis and Schmais (1967, p.112)

Table 3 summarises the interpretative aspect of analysis for each of the four examples used throughout the chapters, those of step dancing, French court and theatre dancing, Tongan dance and *Water Study*.

So far this chapter has identified those concepts through which interpretations of dances may be made and has shown that interpretations may have three identifiable strands, that is, aspects pertaining to character, quality and meaning/significance. The nature of both dance and interpretative activity, however, are such that no single interpretation can be regarded as definitive. This and the fact that interpretations rest not only upon factors relevant to the objective features of the dance, but also the experience of the percipient, make it appropriate to ask what criteria might be used in judging the merit of any one interpretation.

Some ascriptions may be judged in terms of their correctness or truth. For instance, it is the case that *Water Study* has a certain character as it belongs to a particular genre and style, or that some religious dances are concerned with aspects of death. Other ascriptions, however, can only be judged to be *apt* or *appropriate* but not true or correct. For example, qualitative descriptions may rely on an imaginative involvement with the dance, that is seeing the dance *as* something, as, for instance, a 'delicate and sensitive portrayal'. Although the ascriptions of delicacy and sensitivity can be substantiated (or not) with reference to the components of the dance, it is not the kind of ascription which can be proved to be correct nor would it be appropriate to say that it was true.

Thus, interpretations of a dance may be made up of aspects which are open to judgements of truth and correctness and aspects which can only be said to be reasonable, apt or appropriate. The *balance* of these aspects of an interpretation varies according to the dance under consideration. Some dances may be more closely related to factual, actual or prescribed elements than others and are, thus, more appropriately regarded from the standpoint of truth or correctness. The context and purposes of some dances make them such that there is a particular interpretation which, in the main, can be shown to be true or correct. Other dances, especially those which are primarily imaginative and individual constructions, are rightly regarded with a freer and more imaginative attitude and can be understood to have a range of possible interpretations. In the case of most dances interpretation may relate to different levels of understanding and appreciation. It is possible, therefore, that a variety of interpretations may exist which appear to be different and even mutually exclusive.

Overall interpretations can be said to be plausible or implausible according to some criteria which are based upon truth or correctness and others based upon reasonableness and appropriateness.

The plausibility of an interpretation rests upon factors external to the dance and upon the interrelated components of the dance. For instance, Davis and Schmais's interpretation of *Water Study* can be seen to be plausible because, firstly, they state what the dance is about (that is, water in the forms of swells, currents, waves, cascades etc. which are 'low and calm', 'clashing', 'rushes', 'lighter, gentle laps') and they substantiate their statements with particular reference to the movements and clusters of movement components found within the dance. The reasons form adequate and appropriate criteria for the statements. But, secondly, it is also the case that their statements and supporting reasons are in keeping with both the title of the dance and the known and accepted form and behaviour of water. On all of these grounds their interpretation can be said to be plausible.

'Plausibility' is also an important concept in relation to the interpretations of both the choreographer and performers. In the same kind of way these interpretations have elements of correctness and truth and elements of aptness and appropriateness. In the light of all the known factors relating to the dance, the broad setting, and its detailed construction and performance, the interpretations can be said to be reasonable or unreasonable, plausible or implausible.

Thus, interpretations take into account a range and wealth of considerations derived from the socio-cultural background as 'crystallised' in the notions of genre, style, subject matter and treatment. After viewing the dance (or, in the case of the choreographer and performers, in creating the dance) a specific character, a range of qualities, a number of meanings and certain significances are ascribed or attributed to the basic materials and structures (components and their interrelations). Ascribed character, qualities, meanings and significances vary and may be judged true, correct, reasonable or appropriate according to the dance in question. Thus, some interpretations (or aspects of interpretations) are wrong simply because they do not accord with factors that are known to be correct or true and some are right because they do. Some interpretations may be implausible because they are unlikely, in relation to the notions of genre, style, and subject matter and its treatment, or because they cannot be substantiated with reference to the perceptible features of the dance (as they are detailed in Chapters 2 and 3), and some are plausible because they are likely and can be substantiated.

The aim of this chapter has been to show that dance analysis is concerned with much more than the perceptible features of the dance. Whilst the meanings and significance of the dance can *only* be found through direct perception and experience, *access* to the meaning and significance is only possible through a variety of concepts and in the light of certain modes of thinking. The study of dance, which is concerned with interpretation and understanding through analysis, relies upon the openness, receptivity and sensitivity of the person to the features, appearances and effects of the dance but, at the same time, it is firmly rooted in the conceptual structures and modes of thought which make close and discriminating attention possible.

Table 3. Four research examples: interpretations of the dance

---

STEP DANCING: HULME, A-M, and CLIFTON, P, 1978
CLIFTON, P, and HULME, A-M, 1982

INTERPRETING THE DANCE

3.13 *Genre:*
   step dancing of North Norfolk specific to an area 20 miles × 10 miles from the coast inland
   social context of Harvest frolics, Quoits matches, socials and general family get-
   togethers
   occurred with traditional 'Long Dance', polkas, schottisches 'Broom dance' and other forms, gradually replaced by modern ballroom types, e.g. two step, valeta

Table 3 – *continued*

3.131 *style:* 'pure' step dances but three distinctive styles within the category; Norfolk stepping, intrinsic to the area; Travellers' stepping, derived from gypsies and other music-hall travellers; modern Lancashire stepping, derived from an immigrant.
distinguishing characteristics of each type found, e.g. in the use of music of
a different kind, or in lack of heeel beats
individual and family styles exist within each category.

3.14 *Subject matter:*
pure movement using only stepping patterns

3.22 *Qualities:*
lively, vigorous and fun
neat and precise in steps
complex and exciting in rhythm

3.23 *Social statement/meaning:*
exists as a social, family activity in the home and in public houses. Also for competitive purposes

---

TONGAN DANCE: Kaeppler, A L, 1971
Kaeppler, A L, 1972

INTERPRETING THE DANCE

3.13 *Genre:*
Tongan dance genres distinguished by different types of leg movement/range of arm movement and by performers being male or female
there are 6 genres of 3 main types
3 include poetry and music link but are performed on different occasions, i.e. special, formal and informal ones and each uses a different structure

3.131 *style:* several styles distinguished by structure in the use of cadences and a particular range of combinations of action distinguished by subject matter also

3.14 *Subject matter:*
narrative properties of some dances interpret traditional poems, but treatment is allusive and abstract rather than literally representational, stylisation of everyday and ceremonial movement forms the basis of some dances, e.g. 'rainbow' and kava root notions, pure movement as the basis in others

3.22 *Qualities:*
beauty in terms of gracefulness, softness, the 'proper' use of the head

3.23 *Artistic statement/meaning:*
meanings given by choice of movement, all have significance either in relating to something outside the dance or in the beauty of the movement
meanings can be several rather than single, abstract rather than literal, which is also typical of the Tongan language structure.

FRENCH NOBLE DANCE: Hilton, W, 1981

INTERPRETING THE DANCE

3.13 *Genre:*
French dance of the court and theatre in the eighteenth century based on the court of Louis XIV, 1700–35

Table 3 – *continued*

3.131 *style:* NOBLE
general dance types within the genre include entrée grave (complex men's dances), loure/gigue lente, passacailles, minuet, chaconnes, bourrée, rigaudon, forlane (both sexes) character style, e.g. Harlequin
distinctive choreographic styles of Feuillet, Rameau and Tomlinson

3.14 *Subject matter:*
ideals of nobility, serenity, grace and wit treated for performance in social dances in the ballroom where one couple danced at a time
also in theatrical court entertainment which added elaborate costuming to create lavish spectacle using mythological or heroic plots linking scenes of music, dance and verse
a reflection and formalising of established patterns of prevailing social hierarchy

3.22 *Qualities:*
noble and lively, graceful and elegant
contrasting qualities found in different dances of the style, e.g. entrée grave – majestic; sarabande – strong, calm and sustained

3.23 *Social statement/meanings:*
an acknowledgement of the social status of different groups
a demonstration of the role and position of individuals through exhibition of manner
a symbolic acting out of social interaction
a theatrical extravaganza, protagonists vieing in splendour of spectacle.

WATER STUDY: BY DORIS HUMPHREY:
DAVIS, M A, and SCHMAIS, C, 1967
KAGAN, E, 1978

INTERPRETING THE DANCE

3.13 *Genre:*
early modern dance, American in origin but close to the European style through the influence of Mary Wigman

3.131 *style:* one of the first dances in the modern style to be performed without music and to use groups of dancers in a non-metrical way
Hymphrey's personal style recognisable in the giving in to gravity and the rebound away, the fall and recovery principle, also in the non literal nature of the expression

3.14 *Subject matter:*
the waves, the sea and images of water treated in such a way that the movement corresponds to the energies and spatial configurations of water, not in a literal representation of 'spray' etc.
abstract in treatment

3.22 *Qualities:*
swelling and ebbing turbulence within repeated patterns, clash and bursting to a high peak which then subsides in lighter cascades, scattered peaks of water gradually become gentle, lapping waves against the beach flocking and wheeling a 'pulsating gently shifting mass' (Siegel M, 1979, p32)
suspension and mobility arising from spatial stress up and out then dropping vertically

3.23 *Artistic statement/meaning:*
the play of natural forces in water
a poetic image of water

NB In the examples quoted in Chapters 2 and 3 the numbering system parallels exactly that of the chart described in Chapter 6. The explication of examples in Chapters 4 and 5 is given in abbreviated form.
© Adshead, J, adapted from authors' accounts.

CHAPTER 5

Evaluating the dance

by Pauline Hodgens

Concepts through which evaluations are made
Concepts relating to the evaluation of a specific dance
Four research examples

Critical appraisals of dances are generally a mixture of skilfully interwoven descriptions, interpretations and evaluations. For the purposes of analysis and clarity, distinctions between descriptions and interpretations were drawn in the previous chapters, whilst recognition was made of their interrelations and interdependence. Distinguishing between interpretations and evaluations is equally problematic as these, too, are interrelated and interdependent. 'Evaluating', as it is used here, however, is taken to refer to the skills of appraising and judging the merit or worth of the dance.

Concepts through which evaluations are made (4.1)

Although Chapter 6 identifies four distinctive groups of concepts through which evaluations may be made, they are, nevertheless, closely interrelated. For this reason they are not considered separately here. The aim is to point to the aspects of the culture which are the source of the relevant values in relation to which dances are evaluated, and to identify the kind of thing that is valued in the context of dance.

Dancing, in all of its diverse forms, is created and exists within a social and cultural milieu. It is, therefore, inevitable that it is embedded in and shot through with human values which derive from the general values held by the people in question. Each *context*, within which dance appears, carries its own values. Social dances are not valued for the same kinds of reasons as ritual dances, nor ritual dances and social dances for the same reasons as theatre dance. The conventions and traditions of the *genres* and *styles* existing within these contexts are the 'crystallisations' of the relevant values of a given society. They have implicit norms, standards and criteria for what constitutes good performance and good choreography and, therefore, for what might constitute a dance of worth. The norms and standards of classical ballet, for instance, (those associated with, for example, verticality, equilibrium, symmetry), establish specific criteria for what might constitute a good dance in its own terms, and for what ought to be present for the dance even to be considered for its worth. Closely related are values associated with both subject matter and treatment. Certain beliefs, ideas, stories etc. are deemed to be appropriate and important in the same way that certain kinds of treatment have acquired approval.

The norms, standards and criteria appropriate to a particular genre are general and allow a great deal of flexibility. Even working within these constraints there is considerable room for individuality and for manoeuvre. Choreographers may have the freedom to reflect their own values, which, although they have to be in keeping with those mentioned above, may also be markedly individual. Thus, certain criteria for establishing the worth of the dance may also relate to the distinctive values of the choreographer and performers. For example, that which is valued in ballet is different from that which is valued in modern dance. Across the genre of modern dance there are significant value differences between Central Europe and America, while even within American modern dance those of Graham are different from those of Cunningham. Thus each dance embodies and reflects the values of a given society (or group within society), a given choreographer (where relevant) and given performers, and they can be judged for their worth in terms of merit, goodness and greatness, according to whether and how they manifest the given values.

From this brief discussion of values it is not difficult to see why *any* statement about *any* dance must be hedged about by values and value systems. The very concepts which are used to interpret any dance are embedded in identifiable values. Thus, statements which attribute character, quality or meaning often contain evaluative terms or imply evaluations. Sharp divisions between the concepts of interpretation and evaluation are not, therefore, wholly appropriate. Nevertheless, it is assumed in this chapter that the *interests* and *purposes* of interpreting and evaluating can be differentiated. Whilst an understanding of a dance assumes a knowledge of values (for they are part and parcel of both the dance and the spectator's apprecia-tion), statements about the dance may be made without *deliberately* taking them into account.

In this book, therefore, interpreting is used as the overall term for recognising in the dance, and ascribing to it, character, qualities, meanings and significance, things which can be done without direct recourse to comment about the worth of the example. Evaluating is used as the overall term for judging the worth of the dance in terms of its merit, goodness or greatness.

All evaluations assume or state specific values. To say that a dance has worth because it has 'x' features amounts to saying that 'x' features are valued in relation to dance, that this dance has 'x' features, and that, therefore, this dance has worth. The valued features are seen to be enough or more than enough (or not) to warrant and substantiate the judgement of merit. If the dance is compared with others, then the features are assessed in terms of 'more than' or 'most of', and warrant and substantiate the more powerful judgements of good or great.

Having established that there are dance-related values, the next stage is to identify them. Although *particular* values can only be identified in relation to *specific* dances, it is, nonetheless, possible to generalise and to point to *categories* of things which allow us to say that dance has merit or that it is good or great (or not).

Dancing in general, or individual dances in particular, are enjoyed and valued by performers and spectators for a number of very general reasons which reflect three specific (although interrelated) categories of value. These can be described as 'purpose values', 'experiental values' and 'choreographic and performance values'.

Many dances have purposes, aims and intended outcomes which can be specified. When this is the case worth can be assessed in accord with the success or failure of the dance in achieving the purpose. In some instances the purpose may be clear and relate to verifiable happenings outside the immediate dance. For example, in the context of religion or ritual the dance may be directed towards an identifiable and separate outcome such as the onset of a natural phenomenon like rain or to the general fertility of the society. In these cases, the worth of the dance relates directly to the desired and actual outcomes.

Some dances have specific purposes which are both more immedi-ate and more intimately related to the dance at the time of the performance. They are valued for what they achieve and, more obviously than the previous examples, for *how* they achieve it. For instance, dances may exist to celebrate a particular event. In Tonga dance was used to celebrate the coronation of the king and in Norfolk the 'harvest frolics' might include step dancing. In these cases the worth of the dances is judged in terms of their celebratory nature but also in terms of how the dance is created and performed and its appropriateness for the occasion or event.

In the case of many dances in the context of art, questions pertaining to outcomes or 'extrinsic' purposes are not always appropriate. If the notion of purpose has any place at all, it is in relation to the nature of the statement which the dance itself makes. The questions generally asked of these dances relate to their internal features and effects – whether, for instance *Water Study* creates images of water, Tongan dances create beauty, or the dances of the French Noble style demonstrate elegance, wit and grace.

Evaluations based upon values to do with purposes and outcomes rest upon a value structure which is complex. To comment on the worth of, for instance, a specific foxtrot is to make a statement within, and which is reliant upon, an extensive structure. A foxtrot is a style of ballroom dance and ballroom dancing is one genre of social dancing. The worth of the foxtrot thus pertains to its nature as an example (style) of a genre (ballroom) within a form (social dance) of the activity of dance. Dance in general is valued for a variety of purposes and outcomes, social dance is valued for a selected group of purposes, ballroom dance is valued for particular related purposes and the foxtrot is valued for very specific related purposes. Thus the values of the foxtrot are clearly specific to that type of dance but are inter-related to the values of ballroom and social dance.

The evaluations of the foxtrot which relate to purpose may be directed towards different ends, that is to the worth of *any* foxtrot as a social or ballroom dance or to the worth of a *particular* foxtrot *as* a foxtrot. Judgements about the worth of the foxtrot as a ballroom dance would have to take account of the purposes of ballroom dance as distinct from any other genre of social dance, and the purposes of the foxtrot as distinct from any other style. The eventual evaluation would pronounce upon the effectiveness of this particular dance style in bringing about the appropriate ends. The worth of a *particular* foxtrot would be decided on the grounds of all the relevant purposes and whether or not the particular example of the dance achieves the anticipated outcomes.

The same kind of 'purpose value' structure could, in principle, be mapped out for dances in any other context (e.g. art, religion or ritual).

Dances are frequently valued for the *experiences* they engender. They are thought to have worth in as much as, for example, they create interest, enjoyment or pleasure, or they reveal new horizons in thought or awareness. For instance, some Tongan dances, although created and performed for the celebration of a particular event, are partly judged in relation to 'māfana', that is, in relation to the experience of 'inward warmth and excitement'. In the same way dances in the theatre may be judged, in part, for their entertainment value, and dances in the social setting for the enjoyment, entertainment or group cohesion which is experienced. This category of value, therefore, pertains to the *experience* of the dance (which may or may not relate directly to its purposes), in other words to the realisation and experience of the character, qualities, and meanings by the spectator or performer.

It is important to be clear about the nature of the relationship between the experience and the dance. A myriad of experiences *may* occur as the dance is watched or performed and they may or may not relate directly to the dance. Some experiences are initiated, developed and contained by the dance while others are more easily identified as memories, imaginings or fantasies which are further removed from the dance. The *evaluation* of any dance which rests upon experiential values can only be valid or worth consideration, however, if the experience cited related *directly* to the dance. Although the evaluation will be 'personal', in the sense that it has to do with how the *individual* experiences the dance, and although the value which determines the opinion which is expressed resides in the experience, it must be seen to relate directly to the dance. This means that the reasons for the experience, opinion and judgement and found in the features, form, character, qualities, meanings or significance of the dance itself.

There are cases when a judgement begins (and sometimes ends) with the statement 'I like it', the implicit assumption being that the dance is good because 'I *like* it'. If this personal evaluation can be shown to be made in response to certain features of the dance or to its character, qualities or meanings, then the judgement may be shown to be well founded, as it is based upon an experiential value which is grounded in the dance itself. 'I like it', or some such statement, may function as the initial evaluative statement but its appropriateness and validity is seen in the light of the grounds which are used in substantiation.

Dances are valued not only because of the fulfilment of certain purposes or anticipated outcomes or the arousal of a range of experiences but also because of the way these are brought about. In the case of most dances the purposes are inseparable from the *way* in which these purposes are accomplished. In, for example, most ritual or religious dances the procedures, methods and means are specified in detail as a matter of preserved and even cherished tradition. The *efficacy* of the dance may depend upon the correct and appropriate structure and performance. In the case of most forms of dance there are recognisable genres and styles so that in the context of, for example, social dancing, step dance differs from ballroom dance, and within ballroom dancing the foxtrot differs from the waltz. The notions of genre and style specify the general *manner* of executing what could be regarded as merely a selection of basic human movements in terms of how they should be both structured and performed.

There may, however, be a number of different ways of creating and performing within the specified genre and style and this would be the case particularly in relation to dances in the context of art. In these instances there is a greater freedom of choice with regard to the manner of accomplishing the desired end. Within one genre and general style of dance in the context of art it is possible to find creators as diverse as Bergese and North and within the work of one choreographer a number of diverse examples showing a range of style. Having noted this, it is important to point out that the purposes/outcomes and experiences of most dances are inextricably interwoven with the means and manner of accomplishment, and that the apparent separation evident in this writing is for purposes of analysis and added clarity.

Some values used to establish the worth of a dance come, therefore, from the way the purposes, outcomes and eventual experiences are brought about by both the choreography and the performance. These choreographic and performance values are embedded in the notions of genre, style and the range and treatment of the subject matter. They relate directly to the structuring and presentation of the dance. Identifiable genres and styles have implicit norms and standards which can be identified and which specify to some extent how the emergent dances will be choreographed and performed. The 'choreographic values' relate to the choreography in terms of both the selection and treatment of the subject matter and the technical structuring of the dance. The 'performance values' relate to the performances in terms of the technical and interpretative expertise of the dancer(s).

These categories, as they relate to the concepts through which evaluations are made, produce a broad value structure through which this aspect of dance analysis can be understood. In summary it may be expressed as follows. Each context in which dance appears reflects the general values of the society and culture in question. Groups of dances known as genres and styles are 'crystallisations' of the various values which may relate to the purposes of the dance, important experiences of the dance or the particulars of choreography or performance. In the light of this, the range of subject matter and treatment which is appropriate is also specified. The worth of any dance is, therefore, judged according to these values and the particular norms and standards derived from them.

Concepts relating to the evaluation of a specific dance (4.2)

The discussion of the concept 'interpretation' showed that although dances are embedded within the broad socio-cultural life of the peoples concerned and can only be understood through the relevant concepts, they also create character, qualities and meanings/ significances that can rightly be said to be unique. It is also the case that each dance, although embedded in the value system as outlined, creates its own individual values. It is judged, therefore, in relation to both the values that it reflects and those it creates.

Before proceeding it is important to note that *valuing* the dance is different from the process of *evaluating* the dance. There is a considerable difference between saying 'x' features are valued, the dance has 'x' features, therefore the dance has worth, and I value 'x' features, the dance has 'x' features, therefore the dance has worth. It is possible to attribute worth to, for example, Norfolk step dancing on the grounds of the relevant values associated with the genre and the style and yet to say at the same time that it has no worth simply because the values of the dance are not valued by the percipient. Evaluating in this text is understood to rest upon the values associated with the dance and not those values which may be described as more personal.

Judging the worth or merit of any dance (according to the values described), and in particular an assessment of effectiveness and appropriateness, is possible with reference to two aspects of the dance, the choreography and the performance. In the case of choreography the judgements pertain to the appropriate choice of components and structure, and their effectiveness in terms of the character, qualities and meanings they bring into being. In the case of performance the judgements pertain to the appropriateness and effectiveness of the technical competence and the interpretative skills of the performer in bringing about a dance with specific character, qualities and meanings. For instance, *Water Study* can be judged in terms of (among other things) the appropriateness of the set, costumes, and movements in relation to the idea of the dance. Likewise its overall effectiveness can be judged in terms of its creating an interesting and worthwhile interpretation of the idea in relation to the skilfulness of the choreography and the expertise of the performers.

Comparative judgements of this dance with others are likely to focus upon the differences and similarities and upon which dance may be said to be better or the best.

Although the focus of the judgement may be upon either the individual or comparative worth of the dance, it is apparent that each type of judgement is dependent upon the other without necessarily making it explicit. Any judgement upon an individual dance rests, in the final analysis, upon values which are publicly and generally known and which apply to and derive from a number of individual dances. Judgements on the effectiveness and appropriateness of aspects of *Water Study* may be made in relation to the subject matter and how it is treated in the dance but they are also made on the understanding that it is the dance of a choreographer working at a particular moment in the development of modern dance. Without knowledge of modern dance in this form and the associated conventions and traditions, judgements of appropriateness and effectiveness cannot be made. When comparative judgements are made it is also in the knowledge that in some respects dances are incomparable. Although they are embedded in certain practices and traditions, by and through which they can be compared, the specific and particular statement made by the dance is individual and unique. Thus, comparative evaluations may be made about some aspects of the dance in the knowledge that it is an individual work, and evaluations of the individual dance may be made without explicit comparative references but on the backcloth of general values, norms and standards.

It has been made clear that evaluations are *judgements* based upon certain values, and the more important and likely values have been identified. But this has clarified neither the structure of an evaluation nor the procedure for making it. Supposing, for instance, that a statement about a dance says that it is good because it has a clear, rhythmic and spatial structure. If it can be shown that design is valued in the context of the particular type of dance in question, and that it is a significant value, then the judgement that the dance is good may be valid. What is not clear from this kind of statement is whether or not the judgement is appropriate or correct, that is, whether the dance *is* clearly designed. The statement pertaining to the rhythmic and spatial design is an *interpretative* statement and, as such, it has to be shown to be plausible. The onus is upon the person making the judgement to substantiate it by pointing to the reasons for making it. This can be done by referring to the related features of the dance. The design of the dance may be clear because of the simplicity of the stepping patterns and the gestures, the organisation of the dancers on the stage and the developing repetition which builds into a particularly effective climax. The evaluation is dependent upon the interpretation and the interpretation has to be shown to be plausible in terms of the observable features of the dance. Some evaluations do not rely upon interpretations but these too require substantiation. The dance may have been poor because the dancers were inadequate and their technical expertise not sufficient to cope with the complicated shifts of weight and direction which the dance demanded. The reasons for the evaluation of the dance in these terms can be adequately demonstrated and, unlike those dependent upon interpretations, are not open to question. Any evaluations based directly upon the components or structures of the dance can be settled simply by looking again at the performance or the score.

It is therefore, suggested that every evaluation has three important aspects.

1. It relies upon values which may be explicit or implicit.
2. It makes a judgement of worth based upon these values.
3. It includes a substantiation for the judgement.

These three aspects determine the validity and appropriateness of any evaluation.

Whatever values are assumed or are consciously brought to the dance, the spectator may proceed to evaluate in one of two directions – generally procedure is in both directions. Attention may be directed to the evaluation of the components and form of the dance, that is to those aspects identified and discussed in Chapters 2 and 3. They may be judged for their correctness, effectiveness, success and appropriateness. In the case of step dancing or dancing of the French Noble style the steps, or the pattern of the steps, may be judged in terms of their skill, speed, phrasing, complexity or accuracy. If they are found to be correct and effective in terms of how they are executed or placed alongside each other, they may be evaluated as having merit, goodness or greatness. Because they are central to the dance the dance may, on these grounds, be evaluated as great, or the best, good or better than or having merit.

In the second case the attention may be directed to the evaluation of what is in effect an interpretation (not a component or relationship), that is to the value of the dance in terms of the character, quality or meaning it is seen to bring into existence. The character, quality and meaning may be judged for appropriateness, effectiveness and success. A certain step dance may be judged to be effective and successful because it is 'lively' and 'vigorous'. The judgement is substantiated by pointing out the liveliness and vigour with reference to the components and their structuring, in this case to the number and type of steps, the complexity and speed of the phrasing, the rhythms and the relationship to the music. On these grounds the dance may be evaluated for itself in terms of merit or goodness or it may be evaluated comparatively and said to be better than another or the best of a group.

Four research examples

Using Table 4 on pp. 105–106 as a guide, evaluation can be discussed in relation to each of the four examples referred to in the previous three chapters.

The values used in judging the step dancing of North Norfolk come from those of traditional dancing, step dancing in general and of North Norfolk in particular (as far back as 1870). Some values are also related to that which constitutes the style of the family or individual concerned. Judgements are made by the family or people within the area since step dancing exists primarily as social entertainment for the local community and, within that context, as a competitive event at certain festivities and in the local public house.

The choreographic and performance values which are derived from these sources relate to components, their structures and originality, the variety of step patterns, phrasing and rhythm, and the technical competence of the dancer in terms of vigour, accuracy and speed. The judgements are generally related to the degree of complexity, originality and expertise of the single performance. When the dances are competitive and one dancer tries to 'outdo' the other the judgements are based upon the same values and use the same criteria but they are also comparative.

Evaluations are also based upon the spectators' enjoyment (or not) of the specific character and quality (effects and atmosphere) of the stepping. Liveliness, vigour and fun are the general qualities looked for and judgements are substantiated with reference to the components and forms outlined above. On these grounds the dancing may be evaluated singly or comparatively, as having merit, goodness or greatness.

The values used in judging French court and theatre dancing of the Noble style pertain to the French court and theatre of the eighteenth century, the general dance types and the character and choreographic styles.

Judgements were based upon the choreographic values of complexity of structure and performance values of phrasing, rhythm and harmony of the whole, and accuracy, elegance and grace of the dancers. Responses were thus of either approval of the dress, attitudes, manner and behaviour or of mockery if the dance were not performed correctly.

A sense of rhythm and timing extended to the dancers in relation to each other and the dancers in relation to the musicians. In addition the mood and tempi had to be seen to be appropriate to the dance type, for example Galliard or Bourrée. Nobility and liveliness were the overriding qualities valued in performance. A modesty and lack of affectation in dancing pointed to the good breeding of the performer while the complexity and technical difficulty of the steps was concealed in attaining a 'supremely natural' look (Hilton 1981, p. 219).

The values of Tongan dancing stem from the notion of dance in Tonga ('faiva' with 'haka') and its effects, the genre which is used, and the nature of the particular occasion on which the dance is performed. Thus the values are a mixture pertaining to choreography, performance, experience and purpose. These values are balanced differently according to different genres. In relation to some dances the judgements are solely to do with quality – that of 'beauty' – and therefore the prime focus is upon the combination of movement components known as motifs. Most of the motifs are known to the audience who recognise them and, according to the beauty of interpretation and execution, that is the gracefulness, softness and use of the head, they are judged to have created beauty or not and thus to be good or bad. Part of the judgement rests upon the experience of 'māfana' (inward warmth and exhilaration).

In relation to dances within other genres judgements are based upon a complex relation of choreographic, performance, purpose and experiential values. Evaluations take cognisance of:
— judgements of the poetry based upon the originality and interest-ing nature of its 'allusive' narrative,
— judgements of the dance motifs as original and appropriate interpretations of the poetry,
— judgements of the poetry and dance movements, motifs and choreography as appropriate for the occasion (special, formal or entertainment),
— judgements on the beauty and accuracy of the dance motifs and the beauty and aliveness of the performers.
Given that the poetry and the dancing are appropriate for the occasion the audience judge 'mālie', that is how 'well done' it is, on the basis of 'māfana', that is their own response of inward warmth and exhilaration and, on some occasions, according to whether or not they are drawn into participating in the dancing.

'Well done' judgements are based upon the selection of compo-nents of both the poetry and the dancing; the interrelations and form of the components especially between the poetry and the dancing; and the skilfulness and beauty of the performance. But these judge-ments are related directly to the quality of the percipient's re-sponses.

Water Study is somewhat different from the other examples all of which represent a group of dances. The discussion is limited, therefore, to greater generality.

The values used in the judgement of *Water Study* derive from the art form of dance, early modern dance in America, European stylistic influences and Humphrey's personal style.

In the context of art, dances are regarded as unique. Although there are certain conventions related to each genre and style and, therefore, to each dance, they are not totally binding or limiting. The choreographic and performance traditions of Tongan dance prescribe the movement and content (subject) in considerable detail. In the context of art there is more freedom. One of the recognised traditions of art is the breaking and manipulation of rule-like constraints. Although the range of movement and the use of various components may be restricted it is not subject to the severe limitation of, for instance, dancing of the French Noble style or step dancing. There is the possibility of a wide choice in subject matter, how it is treated and for what purposes. Both choreographer and performers have much greater freedoms.

This being the case the values of the genre and style have only a general, but a very necessary, relevance. Those dances which are firmly rooted in given genres and styles are also set firmly against the values for which they stand. But judgements focus upon the dance and the types of values it creates, which, although they relate intimately with the general values, are not obliged to 'match up' in any great detail. Thus evaluations of *Water Study* are concerned with the appropriateness and effectiveness of the choreography and performance in making an overall statement about 'water'. Judgements focus upon the character, quality and meaning brought into being by the dance and state their worth mainly in terms of appropriateness and effectiveness. Judgements of appropriateness and effectiveness are made against the background of genre and style values. What is considered to be an appropriate and effective treatment of 'water' in the mode of classical ballet would not be the same as that which is appropriate and effective in the mode of modern dance.

It is interesting to look at two evaluative statements about *Water Study* and to note the kinds of values to which appeal is made and the types of substantiation given.

The evaluative statements that the dance is 'a truly organic beautifully conceived work' of 'subtle complexity' (Davis and Schmais 1967, p.112) assumes the choreographic values of (deliberately conceived) wholeness and complexity (these may not count as 'values' in, for instance, post-modern dance). They are judged to be present in the work in such measure and intensity that they are 'truly', 'beautifully' and 'subtly' present. These judgements are substantiated by the rest of the article, which studies the style and composition of the dance in terms of level, shape flow, effort flow, group relationships and group formations, all of which are described in considerable detail.

Siegel writing of Humphrey's work in general says that,

> Doris Humphrey had a genius for microcosm. She could reproduce the overall form of the dance within the activity of a small group or the steps of an individual dancer. Her dances fit together like wonderful geometric structures, interlocking, overlapping, reflecting, multiplying, wheels within wheels.
>
> Siegel (1979, p.29)

This is written in the context of a discussion of *Water Study*, which she describes as 'a masterpiece of the choreographic art'.

The value which Siegel identifies is that of 'form', that is form used to create the effect of 'microcosm' and form in terms of 'geometric structuring'. She reveals the form of the dance by a careful description and analysis of the movement and formations and her judgement upon the dance is that it is a 'masterpiece of the choreographic art'.

The difficulty of evaluating a dance of another historic, geographic, social or cultural setting has already been pointed out. But, given that the relevant frameworks can be acquired, evaluations can proceed as outlined. Difficulties also arise with dances which exist in more than one context (for example, religious dances found in the context of art or social dances found in the context of religion) or with dances which fall between or straddle genres and styles. In these cases the range of consideration is more extensive and the number of relevant values increased but in both instances once the frameworks have been recognised and acquired, evaluations are made in the same way. In all of these examples the difficulties do not cast doubt on the sense of evaluating the dance nor do they deny the possibility of valid judgements being made.

Some dances exist as affirmations, rejections, questionings or extensions of previously held or concurrently held conventions and standards. In these cases also there is no insoluble difficulty, the principles and procedures for evaluation are the same but the evaluation rests upon a comparison of the new values with the old, or one set with another. The two sets of dances are examined for the ways (choreographic and performance) in which they achieve the purpose and the range of effects and experiences they bring into being.

When dances are statements of total rebellion and total departure from known values and practices there are increased difficulties. In the case of the American 'Post-moderns' and some of the extreme British 'new dance' the basic fabric of the dance seems to disappear. In the need to create a new medium for new values to emerge, the type of movement, technique, performance space, costume etc. normally considered acceptable, and the notions of what constitutes choreography, performance and spectatorial involvement, are drastically changed. In this context evaluation may have to be suspended; in practice it is certainly severely restricted and difficult. There are no known values, of the type described, to which to relate except those against which the dance rails. These certainly reveal the values *not* embodied in the dance but do nothing to suggest those which might have replaced them.

The basic values in which these dances are embedded can be derived from both the 'creators' of the dance or, in some measure, from the dance itself. The dance uses and structures (or not) specific components in certain ways. These can be discerned and, according to what is both present and absent, it may be possible to decide how the dance is best 'interpreted' and what kinds of interpretation its discernible features might support. In the absence of genre and style 'guidelines' the only other 'information' to which there is recourse is that deriving from the creator or the school of thought from which the dance emerges. The consideration of both what can be discerned in the dance and what the aims of the choreographer and performers are can together lead to some kind of evaluation. The dance may be judged for achieving what it sets out to do, that is whether or not the 'content' and treatment is appropriate and effective for the desired outcome. The only other kinds of judgements which can be made relate to the percipient's response to pleasure, liking or some such personal approval. The dance may give rise to certain experiences, create certain effects, moods or atmosphere because of the way the components are structured and thus perceived.

Evaluation is thus possible but it is somewhat limited. The values which are used are found within the one dance in relation to the unique or new purpose. The judgements are 'internal'. This being the case comparative judgements are not really possible as like cannot be compared with like. In the absence of generally accepted values it is impossible to comment upon the comparative goodness, or merit, of the dance and questions of greatness do not arise.

Questions about comparative merit can only be answered when the dances have gained something of the 'genre/style' structure. Then, values can be identified and the works can be evaluated within the 'world of dance'. It was, perhaps, only in the late 1970s and the early 1980s that the post-modern dance of America could be fully appreciated for what it was and some assessment made of the values it stood for and its overall contribution to twentieth century dance.

This chapter has outlined both what it is to evaluate a dance and what constitutes an evaluation. It is suggested that an evaluation has three important aspects:

— certain values are assumed – purposive, choreographic, perform-ance or experiental.

— judgements are made which relate to the values, and

— reasons and criteria for the judgement which are found in the dance itself are offered.

The dance may be judged to be appropriate and effective in relation to the various values and be pronounced to have individual and/or comparative merit.

Table 4. Four research examples: evaluations of the dance

STEP DANCING: Hulme, A-M, and Clifton, P, 1978
Clifton, P, and Hulme, A-M, 1982

EVALUATING THE DANCE

4.1 *Values:*
    enjoyed by all as a social form
    judged by an audience of peers in competitive situations
    social status influenced by abilities in step dancing

    4.2 *Choreography and performance:*
        made on the spot by the dancer and evaluated in terms of its rhythmic vitality and variations in step pattern within the confines of the 'rules' of the steps

        no two dancers do the same sequence and no two performances by the same individual are identical
        evaluated in terms of technical competence and in ability to 'outdo' the next dancer in rhythmic vigour, accuracy and speed.

TONGAN DANCE: Kaeppler, A L, 1971
Kaeppler, A L, 1972

EVALUATING THE DANCE

4.1 *Values:*
    depending on the genre, for the quality of the interpretation of poetry, for the creation of beauty, for original dance motifs for the occasion, for its effect on spectators in creating 'inward warmth'.

Table 4 *continued*

4.2 *Choreography and performance:*
dances fixed, cannot be changed without destroying the meaning
some newly choreographed ones use the same movement vocabulary and combinations of movements
long established agreement on the suitability of these dances for their purpose
torso movement may be introduced but is not seen as part of the dance
movements taken close to the body are applauded since they are seen to be more difficult
exact timing of movements important

FRENCH NOBLE DANCE: HILTON, W, 1981

EVALUATING THE DANCE

4.1 *Values:*
contemporary response written in terms of dress, attitudes, manners, correctness of behaviour
social mockery accorded for failure to dance correctly

4.2 *Choreography and performance:*
basic repertoire of types of dances remained constant but 2–4 new dances made each year
criteria for evaluating new ones based on complexity of structure and the creation of the 'noble' aesthetic, derived from the French interpretation of classical Greek ideas

correctness of choice of tempo judged by suitability for phrasing, rhythm and harmony of the total performance technique judged in terms of grace and elegance combined with complete accuracy

---

WATER STUDY: BY DORIS HUMPHREY:
DAVIS, M A, and SCHMAIS, C, 1967
KAGAN, E, 1978

EVALUATING THE DANCE

4.1 *Values:*
valued in terms of geometric structuring of form into wholeness and complexity
a piece that has stood the test of time, has remained in Humphrey's repertiore consistently and has been revived many times since her death

4.2 *The choreography and performance:*
long history of critical acclaim since 1928 with such statements as 'a masterpiece of the choreographic art' (Siegel, M, 1979, p.27)

a brilliant, truly beautiful organic work of subtle complexity, 'a masterpiece of flowing motions, full of lighness and grandeur' (King E, 1978, p.21)
performance style requires the giving into gravity and the rebound with intake of breath to produce the distinctive Humphrey style
the movements are usually well-mastered but it is in the interpretative requirements that some performances fail to realise the distinctive style

---

NB In the examples quoted in Chapters 2 and 3 the numbering system parallels that of the chart described in Chapter 6. The explication of examples in Chapters 4 and 5 is given in an abbreviated form.
© Adshead, J, adapted from authors' accounts.

PART II

Dance analysis in practice

CHAPTER 6

Skills and concepts for the analysis of dance

by Janet Adshead, Valerie A Briginshaw,
Pauline Hodgens and Michael Huxley

The theoretical basis of dance analysis
Dance analysis: four stages
Summary

The theoretical basis of dance analysis

The framework which has been outlined in the previous chapters
and which is presented here in the form of a chart is the direct result
of an article by R A Smith and C M Smith entitled 'The artworld
and aesthetic skills; a context for research and development' (*Journal
of Aesthetic Education* 1977, vol.11 no.2, pp. 117–32). The Smiths
argue that aesthetic education is concerned with the creation of a
discerning public who are able to participate in the aesthetic realm.
This done, they maintain, by teaching the basic skills of aesthetic
appreciation. It is the skilful probing of an aesthetic object which
brings about a deeper and a more informed response. They argue
that appreciative encounters with aesthetic objects can be analysed
into something resembling a set of rules, steps or procedures.

A systematic procedure is proposed, layed out in the form of a
chart, including major headings of 'skills', 'concepts', 'anticipated
difficulties inherent in the concepts' and 'anticipated difficulties
based upon misconceptions'. The Smiths identify skills, concepts
and difficulties in order to demonstrate that the notion of aesthetic
education is firmly grounded in an identifiable range of knowledge
and a set of procedures and, therefore, that art appreciation can be
shown to be teachable.

The Smiths make it clear that for illustrative purposes their
scheme is limited to the visual arts but they suggest that a 'task for

research would be to determine the major concepts and skills in other art forms and to find out how much analogy exists' (Smith and Smith 1977, p.126). It was in response to this that we developed and refined their structure in relation to dance studies and created what we now refer to as 'A chart of skills and concepts for dance' (Adshead *et al* 1982). A similar exercise was subsequently undertaken for music (Goolsby 1984).

The version presented here is developed from this earlier account and subsequently amended in the light of further discussion on the theoretical basis. The extended accounts given in Chapters 2–5 reflect the outcome of these debates.

The chart on pages 118–121 is a summary statement of what is involved in analysing dance. In some senses it is a neutral, abstract and conceptualised framework, in so far as it is possible to be neutral, and acknowledging that even the choice of terms, indeed, language itself, is already culture-bound. It is a general and logical structure of both the skills and the concepts necessary for understanding and appreciating dance. It is not constructed out of 'thin air' but, on the contrary, it takes into account both philosophical issues and critical theory and is firmly rooted in examples of dances from different cultures and historical periods and which perform different functions in society.

The chart provides a guide for the analysis of any dance in as much as it identifies the possible range of components and basic structural devices and suggests how, and in what interests, interpretations and evaluations are made. Dance can be described in terms relating to its fabric, form, character, quality, meaning and value. The conceptual framework points to the *nature* and *range* of knowledge which is necessary both for understanding the *meaning* and appreciating the *value* of the dance. It does this in principle, not in detail. Each dance and every performance of a dance is individual and, to this extent, is unique. Its meaning and worth can *only* be discovered and appreciated by attending to the dance itself. The chart allows the spectator to note the selection from the total possible range of components which constitute a dance, i.e. the perceptible features of a particular dance.

Access to the meaning, and assessment of the worth of the dance, however, depends upon the interpretation and the evaluation of these perceptible features. Thus the chart also points to the range of concepts which are necessary for *making sense of* that which is discerned, that is, for attributing to the features character, quality, meaning and value (Stages 3 and 4).

The *dance* chart uses the same taxonomic and hierarchial form as that of the Smiths for the visual arts. In effect it is a structure in four stages for the *analysis of dance* which includes the skills and concepts but not the anticipated difficulties. Each stage is grounded in the stage which preceeds it and, taken together, they show *what* is analysed and, therefore, may be appreciated, and *how* to proceed in the act of dance appreciation in terms of the skills, activities and knowledge structures involved. Dances are created by the manipulation of separately identifiable components. These most basic elements are structured and designed to create a web of relations known as the 'form' of the dance. The dance is understood through the activity of interpreting, thus the perceptible features are characterised and qualities and meanings are ascribed to them. On the basis of an awareness of the components, the form and the interpretation it is possible to evaluate the dance. These four stages in analysing dance reveal the different skills and concepts which are important at each stage and the nature of the relationship between them.

The *skills* of *discerning*, *describing* and *naming* the components and the form of the dance are isolated and identified at Stages 1 and 2. At Stage 3 these skills create possibilities of *recognising* and *identifying* the character of the dance, *ascribing* qualities to it and understanding its meaning. In turn the skills of Stage 4, those of *judging* and *appraising* , become possible.

The *concepts* identified in the chart are similarly interdependent. The concepts relating to the components of the dance are the basic constituents of the web of relations. Concepts pertaining to relationships form the basis for notions of character, qualities and meanings and they, in turn, form the grounds for concepts pertaining to worth and value. At Stages 3 and 4 the chart becomes more detailed because of the complexity of the skills and concepts which are involved. For clarity a distinction is made at these stages between the concepts *through* which and *in relation* to which *any* interpretations and evaluations are made and the concepts relating to the interpretations and evaluations of *specific dances*.

The chart also demonstrates the relationship between skills and concepts, that is, which skills are exercised in relation to which concepts. All of these relationships can be simply expressed in the following form:

STAGES	SKILLS	CONCEPTS RELATED TO
1	discerning, describing, and naming	the components (elements)
2	discerning, describing and naming	the form (web of interrelated components)
3	recognising, ascribing and understanding	character, qualities, meanings, significances (an interpretation)
4	judging and appraising	the worth and merits of the dance (an evaluation)

The chart shows the framework through which important elements of the dance might be located, characterised and evaluated. It does not, however, lay down or imply any particular order of events to be followed in the *process* or *method* of analysis. The structure is logical in that it reveals the grounds for certain types of statements about dance but the logic of the construction does not specify a beginning place or a route.

Dance analysis: four stages

Stage 1

Stage 1 of the chart sets out the four basic components of the dance (movement, dancers, visual environment, aural environment) and complexes of these components. The *movement* component, 1.1 (this numbering system refers to that used in Tables 5–8 on pp. 118–121), which is perhaps the most important, is represented in the greatest detail and shows that analysis may pertain to the type of movement employed and in what particular spatial and dynamic form. Although it is easy to identify each component separately, in the context of an actual dance they appear in clusters of things. For example, a single step may be taken by the right foot which moves in a forward direction (relative to the body) with lightness at a quick pace. Even in this amount of detail, which is far from complete or exhaustive, it is easy to see that a movement comprises a cluster of elements and creates a complicated unit. In principle the same is true of the other four components. They generally appear as a cluster and therefore as a complicated unit of dance.

Although it is possible to discern and analyse each component (or cluster) separately they appear in dances in relation to one or more of the other components or clusters. Thus any analysis has to take into account conjunctions of components and clusters which we have called *complexes*. For example, the step described above might

111

be performed by two dancers who are female and who take, respectively, a major and a subsidiary part in the total dance. The two dancers perform the step in the stage area available within the limitation imposed by three large mobiles lit by a wash of blue and placed in a triangular formation with one at the back of the stage and one at either side. Words are spoken off stage while at the same time random sounds occur from the click of parts of the mobiles against each other. This illustrates that analysis at the most simple level involves attention to the basic constituents of dance which we have termed components (and their many elements) and complexes of components.

In as much as the first stage of the chart identifies the basic constituents of the dance it can be seen to be relevant to the work of the creator, performer, spectator and notator of the dance. It is in relation to the components that each practises additional skills. The *choreographer* creates with them, the *dancer* performs with them, the *spectator* appreciates and describes them and the *notator* records them.

Stage 2

Stage 2 of the chart identifies varied types of relationships which may exist within the total web of relations in a dance. A dance is not a mere collection of components, it is a structured whole. Discernment and knowledge of the components may be the most basic requirement but seeing the *dance* depends upon seeing the components in their relations and interrelations. It is not enough to see, for instance, that there are six dancers, a group of two and a group of four. It is the relationships that are created between and amongst their movements, stage positions and roles which are the crucial factors. Neither is it enough to see the performance area, the position of various objects on the set, the costumes, the colour and intensity of the light; it is their relationships, one with the other, and with the dancers and their movement, which are significant. It is the relationships between and within the components which create the form and the significance of the dance, and it is, therefore, this kind of understanding which begins to reveal the complexity of the work.

Relationships may occur in a number of ways, for example, some occur and are seen at a specific moment. These are the sort which might be captured by a photograph or seen with clarity when a film is stopped at a particular frame. Relationships of this kind, that is, at a *point in time* may suggest very complex, subtle and extensive relationships involving many aspects of the dance. In contrast, however, they may indicate more simple and obvious relationships in which the various components and strands reinforce or echo each other and direct the attention to a significant focal point. Thus, the dance may be analysed vertically, that is at various points in time. A clear parallel to this is the harmonic or chordal analysis of music which is based upon a vertical structure.

Although an analysis based upon relationships at a point in time is complex, dealing with relations *through time* is considerably more so. The same possibilities are present in the category of relations through time but, additionally, there are all the relationships which accrue from one moment following another. Essentially, relationships through time involve a linear or contrapuntal analysis. Movement, dancers and aspects of the visual and aural setting relate to each other through time, that is, by the previous occurrence, or aspect of an occurrence, relating to the next in time or to that which appears much later in time. Although the general term 'development' is a tempting one to use to refer to progress through time it is fraught with difficulties because of the multiplicity of meaning that it carries. Instead we have chosen to name particular relations through time resulting from the use of such choreographic devices as inversion, elaboration etc., and existing forms such as ostinato, fugue or canon. Fundamentally, any one component/cluster/complex may be sustained as it is, be repeated from one moment to the next, or be altered in a number of different ways, for example by adding new elements or by taking away something that was formerly there. The possibilities are endless.

The web of relationships known as the 'form' of the dance results from relationships both in and through time and from *their* interrelations. In the main, it is this interrelation which draws attention to the highlights or the climaxes and suggests those aspects of the dance which have particular significance.

Thus, the relationships within the dance create its structure in terms of the minor and major phrases, units, strands and sections. A consideration of the total dance form is an analysis of the components in relation, the nature of the relationships and the interrelations of all the relationships. Thus at Stage 2 the dance form may be analysed according to the related components or complexes. The total form may be seen in terms of occurrences at any one moment, or through time, or through a further relationship of the moment to the linear progression. In consequence, recurring themes or motifs, for example, may be noticed and climaxes or highlights brought to awareness. It is recognition of this kind which prepares the way for more extensive interpretations.

As Stage 2 is a logical structure for analysing the form of any dance it is of value to the *choreographer*, who, in effect, creates the form, to the *dancers*, who reveal and display the form, to the *spectator*, who detects the form and to the *notator*, whose job it is to record the form on the score.

Stage 3

Stage 3 is primarily concerned with *understanding* the perceptible features of Stages 1 and 2 and thus deals with the skills of interpreting and the nature of an interpretation. At this stage, the concepts *through* which an interpretation is made are identified. The understanding of any dance rests upon extensive knowledge of its location and setting. Dances are social and cultural products which are located within a specific time and place. As such they are directly related to and concerned with the beliefs, knowledge and values of the *socio-cultural background*. Within society and culture dances may exist in a variety of *contexts*, e.g. those of religious, artistic or social life; and they may be associated with many purposes, e.g. therapy, education, worship and entertainment. Thus a certain range of dances may relate to a specific range of knowledge and a specific set of beliefs and values. This knowledge, these beliefs and values, are however, crystallised by and embedded within the more specific concepts of genre and style, concepts which are, in principle, relevant to the dance in any and all of its contexts.

The traditions and conventions of genres and styles prescribe various conditions and procedures for the context, treatment, production and reception of the dance. It is, therefore, only possible to interpret a dance, in a way which is both informed and relevant, through the concepts pertaining to the socio-cultural background and the context. These are more directly described as genre, style, subject matter and its treatment.

The literature pertaining to the arts shows that the terms *genre* and *style* have a variety of meanings. In this text *genre* is used to refer to the forms of dance which are found within a specific context (social, religious or artistic/theatrical). In relation to art and the theatre, it refers to the forms such as ballet, stage dance and modern dance.

114

Each form has specific and distinctive requirements and characteristics and, therefore, the knowledge and recognition of the genre is crucial to an informed and valid interpretation. It would simply be inappropriate to make interpretations of, or statements about, modern dance for instance, using the criteria relevant to ballet or some other form of dance. Examples of a genre are recognised through the use of the skills and concepts described in Stages 1 and 2 since each form of dance rests upon a particular selection from the total range of movement possibilities and relationships available, and presents them in a way which makes a distinctive statement.

Within the various genres there are different general *styles*. Ballet may be in the pre-romantic, classical, romantic or modern style and stage dancing in tap, cabaret or jazz style, for example. Within general styles there are also distinctive choreographic and performance styles. The notion of style rests upon an individual and distinctive use of the components and their interrelations. Styles, like genres, lay down conventions and traditions for the content and treatment of the dance and thus for the selection and use of components and relationships. It is with reference to the perceptual features of a dance that styles are recognised for their individuality.

The conventions and traditions of the context, genres and styles presuppose and, therefore, prescribe specific ranges of *subject matter and the manner of treatment*. At the same time, however, they allow certain freedoms in the selection and use of both content and manner of treatment. Thus, although there are constraints, there is also the possibility of presenting unusual content, treating it in a different way and thereby expressing a different range of ideas and meaning(s).

On the basis of knowing the background of the socio-cultural context and the conventions and traditions of the genre and style which relate to the production and reception of a dance, dances can be understood by recognising their character and ascribing to them qualities and meanings. This overall process of understanding is referred to as 'interpreting' and the solution as an 'interpretation'.

The *character* of the dance pertains to its type and identity, that is, it may be an example of ballet in the modern style as performed by the Royal Ballet of 1981. In addition it may be choreographed by Corder (hence in his own style) and imbued in performance with the individual styles of Sibley and Jefferies. Its subject matter may be identified as well as the kind of treatment which is used. Thus certain conclusions may be drawn about the components which are selected and how they are structured and designed in time and space. This collection of features comprises the character of the dance.

The *qualities* of the dance refer to its appearances, effects, impressions, moods and atmospheres. These qualities are, in effect, the heart or essence of the dance. Ascriptions of quality to any dance are based upon the interest in, and *direct experience* of, the dance itself. They rest upon the discernment of the various interrelated components and on having made sense of them or recognised their character in the light of the background against which they can be located.

Meanings and significances relate to and depend upon the recognition of the character and the range and type of qualities which are ascribed to the dance (with all that these imply). Coming to know what the dance may mean, or its possible significance, is simply a question of bringing together the many facets of character and the range of effects, appearances, impressions, moods and atmospheres which are created. A dance has *this* kind of meaning simply because the associated conventions and traditions make it possible for *this* range of movement and type of relationship to be appropriately viewed as having *this* character and *these* qualities.

In the very broadest terms, then, an interpretation of a dance is the recognition of its character, qualities and, therefore, of its meanings and significances. The *choreographer* interprets an idea, that is, structures and manipulates the components and gives them character, qualities and meanings. The *performer* interprets a role by giving the components and form character, qualities and meanings. The *spectator* interprets the components and the form and ascribes to them certain character, qualities and meanings. In principle all proceed in the same way. Character, qualities and meanings rest upon the selection and structuring of the components according to the conventions and traditions imposed by the genre and style and as appropriate to the context and the creator's aims. Thus the making, performing or appreciating of the character, qualities and meanings is done with reference to precisely the same factors. The *notator* is also concerned with these aspects of the dance in as much as the score has to carry the kind of information which would be necessary for the re-creation of character, qualities and meanings in any subsequent production or reconstruction.

116

Stage 4

Stage 4 is concerned with judging and appraising the dance for its worth or specific merits. At this stage too, the concepts *through which* evaluations in general are made and the concepts used in evaluating an *individual example* are distinguished. Each society and culture has general values which are reflected in particular aspects of life. Thus, the contexts in which dance appears, and the purposes it serves, reflect these values. A genre and style are produced by particular societal contexts so they also embody certain sets of values from the society and culture. In particular they have norms and standards associated with the range of subject matter and types of treatment which may be used.

Evaluations are judgements related to *worth*, that is whether and in what respects dances demonstrate or reflect the norms and standards associated with the particular example. Judgements may focus upon either the choreography or upon the performance of the dance and are generally to do with questions of appropriateness and effectiveness. Evaluations of the performance, for example, pertain to the effectiveness and appropriateness of the technical competence and interpretative abilities of the dancers.

It is possible to discuss the worth of the dance simply because norms and standards do exist in the context of dance. The norms and standards may be varied, they may apply to technical features in detail, they may exist more as principles, they may be rule-like, or they may be more akin to general conventions. No matter what their status, or degree of generality or specificity, they make it possible to judge the worth of a dance and to give reasons for attributing merit or declaring it to be good or great. This being the case they also provide adequate grounds for comparing performances of the same dance, or different dances within the same genre/style, or for comparing different genres, different styles and individual dances within different genres and styles.

Evaluations of the dance, whether they be by the *choreographer, performer, spectator* or *notator*, rely upon the same concepts, are grounded in the same values (norms and standards) and thus proceed in the same general way.

Table 5. A chart of skills and concepts for dance, Stage 1

SKILLS	Discerning, describing and naming components in the dance

CONCEPTS   1   **COMPONENTS**

1.1 *Movement:*
whole body or parts, including actions, gestures, and stillness, e.g. steps, jumps, turns, lifts, falls, locomotion, movement in place, balances.

     1.11 *Spatial elements*
         1.111 shape
         1.112 size
         1.113 pattern/line
         1.114 direction/level
         1.115 location in performance space

     1.12 *Dynamic elements*
         1.121 tension/force, strength/lightness
         1.122 speed/tempo
         1.124 duration
         1.124 rhythm

     1.13 *Clusters of movement elements:* simultaneous occurrence of movement with spatial and dynamic elements (1.1, 1.11 and 1.12)

1.2 *Dancers*

     1.21 number and sex

     1.22 role, lead/subsidiary

     1.23 clusters of elements concerned with dancers, simultaneous occurrence of 1.21 and 1.22

1.3 *Visual setting/environment*

     1.31 performance area, set/surroundings

     1.32 lighting

     1.33 costumes and props

     1.34 clusters of visual elements, simultaneous occurrence of 1.31, 1.32 and 1.33

1.4 *Aural elements*

     1.41 sound

     1.42 the spoken word

     1.43 music

     1.44 clusters of aural elements, simultaneous occurrence of 1.41, 1.42 and 1.43

1.5 *Complexes:* simultaneous occurrence of elements of clusters and/or clusters, i.e. any grouping of 1.1, 1.2, 1.3 and 1.4.

Table 6. A chart of skills and concepts for dance, Stage 2

SKILLS	Discerning, describing and naming components in the dance form. Recognising the comparative importance of relations within the dance form.

CONCEPTS	1	**FORM**

2.1 *Relations according to components:* there may occur within a single
movement or between movements, within a single element or between elements.

    2.11 Relations between spatial and dynamic elements; clusters of movement elements

    2.12 Relations between dancers in number, sex and role; clusters of elements pertaining to dancers

    2.13 Relations between elements of the visual setting/environment; performance area, lighting, costumes and props; clusters of visual elements

    2.14 Relations between aural elements, sound, the spoken word, music; clusters of aural elements

    2.15 Relations between complexes (see 1.5)

2.2 *Relations at a point in time*, i.e. any combination of 2.1

    2.21 simple/complex

    2.22 likenesses/commonalities

    2.23 differences/opposition

2.3 *Relations through time*, i.e. between one occurrence and the next, e.g. between one movement and the next, or one dancer and the next resulting in named relations (canon, fugue, ostinato etc.) and general categories (elaboration, inversion).

    2.31 exact repetition/recurrence

    2.32 alteration of one or more components or clusters

    2.33 addition or subtraction of one or more components or clusters

    2.34 alteration of the order of events

2.4 *Relations between the moment and the linear development* (at a point in time), i.e. relations accounting for particular effects which depend to some extent on a specific moment(s), e.g. emphasis by means of accent, focus, reinforcement, climax

2.5 *Major/minor/subsidiary relations*

    2.51 complexes, strands, units, phrases and sections in relation to each other

    2.52 complexes, strands, units, phrases and sections in relation to the total dance form

    2.53 the total web of relations

Table 7. A chart of skills and concepts for dance, Stage 3

SKILLS	Interpreting the dance: recognising and identifying its character, ascribing qualities to the dance and understanding its meanings.

CONCEPTS   3   **INTERPRETATION**

3.1 *Concepts through which interpretations are made*

    3.11 *Socio-cultural background*, e.g. giving rise to the notion of Tongan dance of the mid twentieth century; located in time and place (historical/geographical)

    3.12 *Context:* purposes of the dance, e.g. for artistic, social or ritual functions, giving rise to the terms social dance, ritual dance etc.

    3.13 *Genre:* grouping dances according to shared characteristics identifiable within the context and socio-cultural background, e.g. ballet; modern dance, as types of dance as art

        3.131 style: of the dance: groupings of dance within a genre exhibiting a smaller range of shared characteristics, e.g. central European/American, as types of modern dance

                style: of the choreographer: e.g. within contemporary dance in Britain 1970–80, the work of Alston, Bruce, Cohan, Davies, North

                style: of the performance: individual style e.g. Odette/Odile by Fonteyn, Makarova; company style e.g. North's 'Troy Game' by LCDT, Royal Ballet and Dance Theatre of Harlem

3.14 *subject matter*

    3.141 content, e.g. 'pure' movement, story, theme, topic or idea

    3.142 treatment e.g. representational, narrative, literal, abstract, lyrical, impressionistic

3.2 *Concepts relating to the intepretation of a specific dance*

    3.21 character: identification of the dance as a specific example of a type of dance through recognition of the subject matter and its treatment, its genre and style, in the appropriate context and socio-cultural background.

    3.22 qualities: ascriptions to the dance of qualities pertaining to appearances, atmospheres, effects, impressions, moods, arising from the character of the dance

    3.23 meanings/significance: understanding of the unique statement or point of the dance through consideration of its individual character and qualities in relation to its purpose or function.

NB Character, qualities and meanings are recognised with reference to components, clusters and complexes as related in phrases and sections of the whole dance. Particular ascriptions of character, quality etc. may relate to parts of the dance or to the whole.

Table 8. A chart of skills and concepts for dance, Stage 4

SKILLS	Evaluating the dance: appraising and judging its worth and merit.

CONCEPTS 4 **EVALUATION**

4.1 *Concepts through which evaluations are made*

    4.11 *The general values of the society and culture*

    4.12 *The specific values embodied in the context in which dances appear* and of the functions or purposes that they serve, as artistic, social or ritual works

    4.13 *The particular values associated with different genres and styles,* reflected in the criteria of excellence (norms and standards) in each sphere

    4.14 Subject matter

        4.141 appropriateness of the range of subject matter found in dances which are characteristic of genres and styles

        4.142 appropriateness of the range of treatment of the subject matter

4.2 *Concepts relating to the evaluation of a specific dance*

    4.21 *Worth and merit of the dance:* that is, how the dance is judged to demonstrate and create both the values associated with the socio-cultural background and context and the norms and standards inherent in the specific genre and style in which the dance is located

        4.211 *Effectiveness and appropriateness of the choreography,* i.e. the choice of components, the structuring of components in relation to the subject matter, style and genre in creating a dance of character, quality and meaning

        4.212 *Effectiveness and apropriateness of the performance,* i.e. the execution of the choreography in a particular instance in terms of technical competence and interpretative abilities in performing a dance of character, quality and meaning

NB Judgements and appraisals of dance relate to the merit and worth of the individual dance. They may also be comparative, that is, the dance may be assessed in relation to other performances of the same dance and other dances which have similar characteristics.

Summary

The overriding reasons for the construction of the chart were to
— locate basic skills and concepts for the appreciation of dance and
— to create a tool for the analysis or 'skilful probing' of specific examples of dances.

If each individual dance can be probed skilfully or analysed for its components, structural devices, character, quality, meaning and value then it is possible to use the chart to compare
— one dance with another in relation to its components, devices, character, quality, meaning and value

— the score with the performance of the dance

— groups of dances, to note like and unlike features.

This makes possible a statement of what characterises a style or genre, and consequently the location of new dances within appropriate styles and genres.

CHAPTER 7

Analysis of variation in choreography and performance: Swan Lake Act II Pas de deux

by Valerie A Briginshaw

Interpretations of *Swan Lake*
Concepts relevant to an interpretation of *Swan Lake*
The Pas de deux from Act II
Analysis of two interpretations of the Pas de deux from Act II, by choreographers' and directors', dancers in the roles of the Swan Queen and Prince Siegfried, and film producers.

The complexity and importance of the notion of interpretation in dance has been thoroughly examined in Chapter 4, where it was stated that the term might apply to the choreographer's interpretation of the subject matter, the dancer's or company's interpretation of the dance and written or verbal accounts as in, for example, the spectator's interpretation. In Chapter 7 different strands of the complex concept of interpretation are drawn out in relation to *Swan Lake*. The focus is particularly on the choreographer's and/or director's interpretations and the dancers' interpretations evident in different versions, productions and performances of the ballet. For the present purposes, *versions* of a dance are distinguished by changes in choreography and different *productions* are characterised by other alterations such as those evident in set or costume, staging or direction.

The analysis of *Swan Lake* is preceded by two introductory sections, the first dealing with interpretations of *Swan Lake* arising from different versions, productions and performances, and the second considering some of the concepts through which these interpretations are made. The latter requires reference to the ballet's origins, its status as an example of a dance of a specific genre and style and the subject matter and its treatment, particularly within the Act II Pas de deux. The analysis forms the major part of the chapter and centres upon a comparison of a filmed and a televised production of the Pas de deux. This example shows how the analytic framework can aid a comparison of different interpretations: those of directors, choreographers and performers. Conclusions are then drawn regarding overall differences of interpretation and the importance of the socio-cultural background.

Interpretations of Swan Lake

There are over seventy different choreographic *versions* of the ballet *Swan Lake*.[1] Almost all are based on the choreography by Petipa and Ivanov (1895) and some versions (e.g. the Royal Ballet in 1979 see Table 9 on p.138) are hybrids of former versions or productions. The two examples selected for analysis and comparison here are the 1959 film, entitled *The Royal Ballet* and produced by Paul Czinner, which includes excerpts from *Swan Lake* Act II, and the 1980 Thames Television production (subsequently made available on videotape) also performed by the Royal Ballet. The filmed production of *Swan Lake*, revived and staged by Ninette de Valois, is the 1952 Ashton and Sergeyev version. The televised production is directed by Norman Morrice with additional choreography by Ashton and Nureyev, and it is a production of the 1979 version for the Royal Ballet (see Table 9). Thus the examples chosen illustrate different interpretations offered by directors, choreographers and performers.

Performances of a dance by the same cast may vary from night to night and from theatre to theatre but the differences are not likely to be as great as when different dancers perform. In the two examples chosen, the year and the performers are different although the place is constant. In the 1959 film Margot Fonteyn and Michael Somes lead the cast whereas Natalia Makarova and Anthony Dowell star in the 1980 televised production. Both performances take place at the Royal Opera House, Covent Garden.

The changes in interpretation that occur with different versions, productions and performances of a dance are such that the genre and general style of the dance are not likely to be affected but the

---

1. See Table 9 for a selection of productions and versions.

124

specific choreographic and performance styles may well be. The subject matter is unlikely to change substantially but it may be altered slightly. For example, some versions of *Swan Lake* end with Odette and Prince Siegfried throwing themselves into the lake and other versions with them reappearing in a fairy barque being drawn over the lake. The treatment of the subject matter might change in different versions, productions and performances and this in turn will affect the character of the dance and its meaning. However, there remains a common core of meaning despite different versions, productions or performances that enables us to recognise the dance as *Swan Lake*.

Concepts relevant to an interpretation of Swan Lake

The two versions of *Swan Lake* examined here are based on the Petipa/Ivanov 1895 version. Petipa was, at the time, the chief ballet master for the Russian Imperial theatres and a renowned choreographer; Ivanov his assistant. In the creation of *Swan Lake* Petipa worked mainly on Acts I and III and Ivanov on Acts II and IV. Petipa's style and treatment of subject matter is often regarded as 'classical' whereas Ivanov's is considered to be more 'romantic'. Petipa was French and Ivanov, Russian, and their contributions are said to reflect these national styles (e.g. Beaumont 1952, p.18).

Swan Lake's nineteenth-century Russian origins, which are relevant to any interpretation of the ballet, are often alluded to by the critics. For example, Clarke writes of a Royal Ballet performance by Fonteyn: 'her body is not an ideal instrument for the Kirov-type choreography devised by Nureyev' (Clarke 1963, p.340). She also laments the fact that the corps de ballet have not got 'Kirov backs and arms' (*ibid*). This would not of course have been a criticism of original performances of the ballet. It is only relevant because of the change in dancers and the time and place of the performance.

When twentieth-century English versions of a nineteenth-century Russian ballet are analysed, knowledge of the socio-cultural context of Tsarist Russia, of the place of ballet within that period and society, of its reception by contemporary audiences and of the appropriate genre and style are all relevant to the interpretation as well as knowledge of a similar kind pertaining to England in the twentieth century.

The Pas de deux from Act II

The second act of *Swan Lake* contains an important part of the narrative because it establishes and characterises the romance between the hero, Prince Siegfried, and the heroine, Odette, the Swan Queen. The Pas de deux between the two main characters provides an opportunity for insight into their relationship. The relationship is of crucial importance, especially for Odette, whose freedom and life depend on Siegfried's love and his ability to keep his promise of marriage. The Pas de deux, therefore, is pivotal to the ballet as a whole and it is generally agreed that Ivanov's choreography effectively underlines its important status. Its importance is evident in the choreographic structure of the act. Since the Pas de deux is the longest section, and is placed centrally, it forms the climax of the act.

The choreography of the Pas de deux centres mainly around the use of developpés, arabesques, lifts, pas de bourrées, pirouettes and fouettés. Consequently the expressive interpretation of individual dancers becomes all-important if the appropriate mood, atmosphere and meaning that give the duet character are to be conveyed. As Gray states of Odette's role:

> from the start she must convince everybody that she is half-swan, half-girl; that she is a princess; that she is humanly in love with Siegfried; of her hope of salvation in his love; and of her ever-present fear of the magician Rothbart. This is not always easy to do in arabesques and bourrées.
>
> Gray (1952, p.46)

Analysis of two interpretations of the Pas de deux from Act II

The two versions of *Swan Lake*, although both by the Royal Ballet, were performed in 1959 and 1980, twenty-one years separating them. This space of time probably precludes any of the same performers from dancing in both, but various people provide links between the two and between them and the original. Both versions are to some extent based on the first full production for the Vic-Wells Ballet in 1934 by Sergeyev. He constructed this from the Stepanov notation of the original 1895 version with which he was familiar since he supervised the repertory at the Maryinsky Theatre then. Both the 1959 and the 1980 versions have additional choreography by Ashton. Michael Somes (Prince Siegfried in the 1959 film) helped to supervise the 1980 television production.

Interpretations by choreographers and directors

It is likely that major changes in interpretation, such as those in the subject matter and the characters involved, are effected by the choreographer or director. Even if the choreography of the Pas de deux remains constant its interpretation is affected by the narrative context in which it is set. In this comparison, since the 1959 film is only of excerpts from Act II, attention is focussed on that particular section of the story rather than seeing the Pas de deux in the context of the full-length narrative.

The characters differ in the two examples analysed here; Benno plays an active part in the Pas de deux of the film whereas he is absent from the television production. He supports Odette in an arabesque at the beginning of the Pas de deux and catches her when she falls a little later and again at the very end. Apparently Benno was originally given a supporting role by Ivanov because the dancer who was to play Prince Siegfried, Paul Gerdt, was fifty-one years old and 'could no longer ... support the ballerina with any degree of strength' (Slonimsky 1959, p.51). Benno's assistance provided the obvious solution, although in a love duet such as this, Benno's intervention might be considered inappropriate, hence his absence from the later version.

Other changes made by choreographers or directors in the basic components are evident in the visual setting or environment. The set and costumes in both productions are attributed to Leslie Hurry and appear very similar. The major difference is the introduction of short, classical tutus for the corps de ballet in the later production whereas, in the 1959 film, Romantic mid-calf length skirts are worn. Both sets consist of naturalistic backcloths of a lake surrounded by trees with the ruined chapel to stage left. However, the 1959 set appears more surrealist in style with heavier, darker rocks and trees around the lake and chapel.

Few special lighting effects are used in either production. There is little attempt to create a romantic moonlit atmosphere, instead the lighting is full throughout so that all the movements of the corps de ballet can be seen. The only difference is that in the 1959 film two large spotlights follow the movements of the principals. This makes very little difference to the overall impression – the production just appears slightly more staged and artificial. Although the differences in visual setting between the two productions are comparatively slight, different effects and atmospheres are produced and these contribute towards the qualities of the two versions and hence the interpretations.

In the following section major changes in the dance movements that seem more substantial than individual performance differences are identified, although further research and analysis would be needed in order to be conclusive about this. These differences occur in the overall pace or speed of the Pas de deux, certain of the Swan Queen's actions and relations between the movements of the two dancers, for example a series of lifts.

One of the most noticeable differences between the two versions is the speed of the dance. This is quicker in the 1959 film, which is between half a minute and a minute shorter than the seven-minute television version. A variation as substantial as this, involving a different tempo for the music, seems likely to be the director's choice. The slower pace of the 1980 production, although evident throughout, is most marked in the duration of particular movements of the Swan Queen (see pp.132–133). The impression of a slightly more tortuous and less passionate growth in the relationship in the 1980 version is indicated by its slow, drawn-out, almost indulgent character.

Another variation which appears substantial involves a change in the choreography in the second half of the Pas de deux when Odette leaves Siegfried and is drawn towards the ruined chapel inhabited by Rothbart. This is a relation between a complex of spatial elements and dancers. In the 1959 version the Swan Queen, facing the chapel, moves towards it and only when she almost reaches it does she turn back and gesture towards Siegfried, who has moved downstage right, and run back to him. In the later version Odette walks a few steps backwards towards the chapel and arches her back, gesturing towards it without turning away from Siegfried or moving far from him, and then she returns to him. The implications in the 1980 production might be that Siegfried has more power over Odette than Rothbart or that Odette is less impulsive and more sure in her relationship with Siegfried.

Choreographic changes result from Benno's presence or absence in the Pas de deux. In the 1959 film when Odette enters she performs an arabesque holding Benno's extended arm before running further forward to arrive in front of Siegfried. The equivalent arabesque in the 1980 production is unsupported. Another choreographic difference occurs at the very end of the Pas de deux: in the 1959 version Odette falls to her right over Benno's knee whereas in the 1980 production she falls to her left over Siegfried's arm and then finishes with an arabesque penchée.

These choreographic changes in the 1980 version, prompted by Benno's absence, tend to give an impression of a more unidirectional, and hence stronger, relationship between the Prince and the Swan Queen. The interpretation may also be regarded as a more modern picture of a relationship since Benno might be seen as a chaperon figure in the earlier production.

The remaining differences in the choreographers' or directors' interpretations concern relations between complexes of components. For example, in the 1980 version when the swan maidens first interrupt the duet, Siegfried and Odette walk towards the back of the stage where they stand together masked by the corps de ballet who are crossing in front of them. However, in the earlier version they do not walk back but merely stand together in the centre whilst the swan maidens cross in front of them.

An example of a difference in the relations through time follows immediately when Siegfried and Odette move forward, both facing the audience, and the first series of lifts begins. Siegfried lifts Odette in front of him whilst she does a développé to the right side and then in the second lift to the left. In the 1959 film version there are nine lifts altogether; a set of three followed by a pair, and when the sequence is repeated, two pairs of lifts replace the set of three and the pair. In the 1980 version however there are only five lifts in all; a pair followed by one then two single lifts when the phrase is repeated. The smaller number of lifts in the later version fits more aptly with the slower tempo of the production overall. These variations alter the form of the choreography using either exact repetition or repetition with the direction altered. However, the form is changed only slightly because the difference is in the number of repetitions rather than in the pattern of repetition; the 3:2 2:2 format is replaced with 2:1 1:1 in the later production.

A similar event occurs in the following series of lifts, when Siegfried carries Odette downstage right from the ruined chapel and then across the front of the stage. In the 1959 version there are three lifts, which are replaced by two in the 1980 version. Whereas in the latter version the Prince travels and turns carrying Odette through the air, in the 1959 production he remains stationary for the first two lifts and only travels in between them and across the front of the stage for the third lift. Aesthetically the 1980 interpretation seems to work better because the flow of movement is continued rather than arrested, thus the pattern of movement is clearer and more harmonious, reflecting a parallel harmony in the relationship being portrayed.

These two series of lifts are strands or units of choreography which, when seen in relation to each other in the Pas de deux, can be recognised as relations of major importance in the duet. Another important strand is the movement of Odette along the diagonal from Rothbart's chapel to downstage right towards or with, Siegfried. This represents spatially the pull of Odette between the two males. Other strands such as the arabesques and développés of the Swan Queen in the first section of the Pas de deux and the pirouettes and fouettés towards the end can be seen as minor relations in comparison. However, some of these strands gain significance when seen in relation to the total dance form, since the arabesques and other movements characteristic of Odette are reiterated in the Pas de deux between Siegfried and Odile in Act III and then again in Odette's dancing in Act IV. These relations in the choreography serve to link the characters of Odette and Odile, giving credence to the Prince's attraction to Odile.

Different interpretations have been identified by discerning differences in components or relations between components in the two versions of the dance. However, because of the nature of this particular dance, focussing on a deeply emotional relationship between two people, the interpretations of the individual performers are elevated to a special level of importance.

Interpretations by dancers

The Swan Queen – Margot Fonteyn and Natalia Makarova

The importance and degree of expressive interpretation required of dancers who play the role of Odette, the Swan Queen, has already been intimated. The dancer has to convey Odette's dual bird/human nature, her regal status, her love for Siegfried and her hope of freedom through him tinged with anxiety concerning her fate. The choreography cleverly and subtly includes bird-like gestures, especially of the arms and head, which are evident particularly in the

130

first part of the Pas de deux but gradually disappear as the duet progresses. The human aspect of Odette's character is inherent in her emotions, which are torn between love and fear. Odette's 'ache for the certainty of happiness and her despair at the certainty of her plight' (Gray 1952. p.49) need to be conveyed. It is the tortuous fluctuation between these two extremes that seems to be the key to the interpretation of the role.

Margot Fonteyn made her debut as Odette in *Swan Lake* in 1936 and had over twenty years experience of the role, in more than one version, before the Czinner film was made in 1959. Natalia Makarova made her debut in *Swan Lake* for the Royal Ballet, in 1972, just eight years before the television production, although she probably danced in many Russian performances of the ballet prior to that. Both dancers are noted for the special contributions they have made to this famous role.

Beaumont considers that the length of time Fonteyn has had in the role is crucial to the depth of her interpretation, which, he states,

> is the outcome of years of constant study, thought and application all directed to the evolution of what was at first no more than a sketch into a complete and finished portrait. . .Fonteyn has not only lived the role but even penetrated the soul of it.
>
> Beaumont (1952, p.156)

Indeed, Fonteyn is often claimed to be one of the few dancers who could successfully dance the contrasting roles of both Odette and Odile equally well. In Beaumont's book on *Swan Lake* Fonteyn is singled out for special mention and praise:

> Russia apart, the finest rendering of Odette to be seen . . . today is that of . . . Fonteyn . . . in which each step and every moment are so invested with meaning and mood that they contribute to the evocation of a most haunting and lyrical portrait.
>
> (*ibid*)

Acknowledging the ballet's Russian home, the importance of Russian interpretations of the work cannot be overlooked. When Makarova first danced the role for the Royal Ballet in 1972, Bland stated that

131

her interpretations [of both *Giselle* and *Swan Lake*] aroused enormous interest, ranging from wild fervour to disapproval. She made few, if any, concessions to the Royal Ballet style: her performances were memorable for her very individual manner – unmistakenly Russian but with an accent all her own.

Bland (1981, p.178)

The importance of both company and individual performance styles which are rooted in a dancer's background, nationality and training, is evident here.

When analysing Fonteyn's and Makarova's performances and focusing on the components, the slower speed of the 1980 version, often a characteristic of Russian interpretations of the classics, is particularly obvious in the duration of certain moments in Makarova's performance. She appears to languish in and draw out every possible ounce of Odette's feelings, torn between hope and despair. Every single développé and arabesque, especially the arabesques penchées, are elongated in this way. This appears to be partly a mark of Makarova's peerformance of this role rather than entirely the director's interpretation since, in a different version of the ballet for American Ballet Theater, Siegel says of Makarova:

in the adagio she stretched and curved along the slowest possible thread of energy

Siegel (1977, p.12)

Fonteyn's performance is speedier, particularly in the pirouettes and fouettés, which come towards the end of the duet. Fonteyn appears to perform a greater number of fast, whipping turns and to perform them more quickly, conveying a more passionate and desparate mood, which contrasts with Makarova's considered intensity.

The two performances provide instances of the comparative importance of different strands in relation to each other. In Makarova's interpretation Odette's feelings seem to be conveyed most clearly in the phrases of elongated arabesques and developpés which assume greater importance, whereas in Fonteyn's performance the pirouettes and fouettés appear to have more emphasis, stressing the ecstatic elements of the relationship.

Another component indicating different interpretations is the comparative shape or line achieved by the two dancers. Makarova's lengthened arabesques penchées stand out in her performance creating a purer, almost vertical line with her leg extension whereas Fonteyn's leg is never higher than approximately 20° from the vertical. The emotional torture of the pull between the two extremes is appropriately conveyed in the physical torture and tension exhibited in Makarova's fully extended limb. It should be noted that there was greater emphasis on technical training in Russia in the 1970s and 1980s than in England in the late 1950s. In the context of the dancers' technical and physical capabilities it is relevant to note that at the time of these performances both women were coincidentally in their fortieth year.

A further example of differences in shape is evident in a comparison of the dancers' execution of another step: a high, open, retiré devant with the head down, one of the few bird-like movements that comes in the second half of the duet. Whereas Makarova stretches herself to the limits in the arabesques penchées, she only slightly indicates a forward bend of the torso and head merely hinting at the swan-like gesture in the retiré devant. In contrast Fonteyn gives a much clearer bird image, sinking her head into some imaginery water. It might be argued that at this later stage in the dance less emphasis on the swan characteristics and more on the human, emotional qualities of the role is more appropriate in the context of the developing relationship with Siegfried. Conversely, a clear recourse to Odette's earlier form at this point might express more accurately her anticipation of her plight. Each interpretation is equally valid if it is consistent with the rest of the performance.

To appreciate the performances fully it is necessary to see them in context and to consider the dancing of Prince Siegfried by the two male partners.

Prince Siegfried – Michael Somes and Anthony Dowell
The role of Prince Siegfried, particularly in the Pas de deux, is often regarded as a typical example of a cavalier role, where the man's function is to show his partner off, support her and be in devoted attendance. In this situation, although the male's responsibility appears much less in comparison with that of the female role, it is important for the character to appear sincere and for the dancer to avoid the pitfall of presenting a mechanical, purely functional, cardboard figure who merely provides the right hand in the right place at the right time! As Beaumont states:

the interpreter of Siegfried . . .needs to be both graceful
and manly, a fine mime with a sensitive appreciation of
style-atmosphere . . .The spectator must share in Siegfried's wonderment at the first appearance of Odette, his
growing admiration, his sympathy for her fate, the dawn
of his love and so on.

Beaumont (1950, pp.24–5)

Anthony Dowell is generally regarded as a fine example of a
'danseur noble', described by Kersley and Sinclair as 'a tall dancer
of fine appearance and good manners towards his partner' (1973,
p.49) and by Koegler as 'the born aristocrat among today's ballet
princes' (1977, p.164). Support for these claims can be found in
Dowell's performance.

Certain qualities may be ascribed to the dance on the basis of
Dowell's appearance. The first hint of sincerity Dowell brings to the
role can be seen immediately before the Swan Queen's entrance
when the Prince is searching for her among the swan maidens.
Dowell shows concern in his face as he searches for Odette and when
he hears the harp notes that herald her entrance he stops immediately, listens and turns to behold her. Somes does not have quite the
same opportunity to capture the audience's attention at this moment
since he is joined in his search by Benno. Even so the impression of
sincerity and concern that Somes is able to muster is somehow less
convincing because his face in particular, but also his body, is not so
expressive as Dowell's, which seems to be reaching out for Odette.
The intensity of expression of Dowell's Prince Siegfried continues
throughout the Pas de deux. He conveys a sense of tenderness, care
and concern for Odette through his gaze, which follows her every-
where, often meeting hers, in his facial expression and his posture.
Somes' performance in comparison, although not 'cardboard', is not
noteworthy. Any further analysis and interpretation of the Prince's
performance is difficult in isolation from that of his partner since the
relations between the two are the *raison d'être* and core of the Pas de
deux.

Partnerships – Fonteyn and Somes; Makarova and Dowell
The Pas de deux is built round a series of relationships between the
two partners. These develop choreographically in the form of the
dance and in the emotional interpretation given in performance.

Emotional links often appear stronger in Makarova and Dowell's interpretation than in that of Fonteyn and Somes. This is mainly due to Dowell's interpretation and some choreographic differences evident in relations between the dancers. For example, in the middle of the Pas de deux, after the first series of lifts, Odette moves away from Siegfried using a pas de bourée step and a retiré to the back. Often the Prince stands and watches Odette at this point waiting for her return. Neither Somes nor Dowell stand and watch, but whereas Somes merely takes a step in the direction in which Odette has gone, Dowell follows her, keeping his distance, portraying a touching sense of affection and involvement.

The impact of differences in the second series of lifts when Siegfried carries Odette across the stage has already been noted. Apart from the different number of lifts (three by Somes and two by Dowell) and the fact that Somes' first two do not travel, whereas Dowell's do, there are marked differences in the relationship between the two partners in each case. When Dowell lifts Makarova he raises her high enough in front of him for her to arch her back over his head and shoulders, presenting a spectacular curved shape in the air. Somes does not lift Fonteyn above his chest, thus limiting her to a flat, two-dimensional pose.

The positions that Makarova is able to achieve are much more fluid and look easy and natural. A sense of flexibility is conveyed in the image which relates more closely, for instance, to the curves of a swan's neck. Fonteyn's positions in the air in comparison appear stiffer, more artificial and rigid. However it is the combinations of all these components in the clusters and complexes presented that convey the nature of the partnership. The smooth, travelling, but secure support that Dowell provides underneath his partner allows Makarova's movement to flow naturally through the air. This conveys a sense of confidence in the partnership between Odette and Siegfried which allows for a parallel image of their relationship reaching heights of ecstacy. The very different complexes of components in the Somes/Fonteyn lifts cannot convey such strong qualities.

The examples of components and relations between components in the partnerships described begin to provide reasons for the suggestion that Makarova and Dowell's interpretation conveys stronger emotional links.

The most significant differences between the two examples analysed are due to the different interpretations of performers, directors and choreographers. However, there are further production differences which, unlike those already considered, are easily distinguishable from version differences. These are the differences between the filmed and the televised productions, partly due to the technical idiosyncracies of the two media and partly to the decisions of the producer involved. They are discussed last because in this instance the differences in interpretation are relatively insignificant compared with those of the performers and directors.

Interpretations by film producers

Film and video are different media produced in different ways. However, since both the recordings of *Swan Lake* studied here are of a performance at the Royal Opera House, Covent Garden, the conditions and requirements are similar and the technical differences that result are minimal. There is some camera movement evident in the television production, for instance, when the camera occasionally follows the movements of the Swan Queen or the two principals but this is relatively rare and hardly noticeable in comparison with the filmed production. Although both are filmed in colour the Thames Television production is more accurate and naturalistic than that of the Czinner film, possibly due to technical improvements in colour reproduction over time.

The action throughout is seen almost totally from the front of the auditorium except in the 1959 Czinner film when the first series of lifts is filmed partly from the side in the wings. The difference is very slight because it only occurs at this point and, if anything, the effect is to break the continuity slightly by focusing on the technical feat and height of the lifts as distinct from their contribution to the overall statement of the Pas de deux. Otherwise the two interpretations are almost identical.

The productions include a mixture of *long distance shots*, where the whole of the stage is in view, *medium distance shots*, where part is in view, and *close-up shots*. The fact that both producers have chosen to use these particular distance or close-up shots for virtually the same sections or moments in the dance seems to point to the strength and clarity of meaning conveyed by the original choreography. For example, both productions give close-ups of the Prince when he is searching for the Swan Queen amongst the swan maidens and when he raises the Swan Queen from the ground. The close-up shot is also used consistently when Siegfried embraces Odette from behind and sways her gently from side to side (sometimes known as the 'wrap around'). This use of the close-up emphasises the comparative importance of relations within the dance since the 'wrap around' is a complex or unit that can be seen in relation to the total dance form (in the 1980 production) because it is established through repetition in the Pas de deux and it recurs in Acts III and IV when Siegfried encounters first Odile and then Odette again. Throughout the rest of the dance distance shots are consistently used when the corps de ballet are dancing and medium distance shots for dancing by the two principals.

The major differences in the two examples of the Pas de deux from Act II of *Swan Lake* examined here lie in the overall *speed* of the two versions, the *relations* between the two principals and in the *individual interpretations* of the roles of the Swan Queen and Prince Siegfried. Not all the differences have been considered but the potential depth of study has been indicated. By describing the differences in interpretation an attempt has been made to trace them to some of the *components* and *relations between components* evident in the two danced examples in the context of the analytic framework. Despite the myriad differences, some substantial and some minute, it is also the similarities of the two examples, although not considered here in any detail, that are important to a full understanding of the interpretations given. The similarities outweigh the differences and provide a common core of choreography in the Pas de deux which makes comparisons of interpretations possible. The choreographic strength of the Pas de deux lies in its use of a number of different steps that are consistent and appropriate within a particular *genre* and *style*. It is this stylistic coherence, embodied in the combinations of steps, the relations between them and other components such as the music, that result in the dance having a certain *character* and effectively conveying unique *qualities* and *meanings*.

Changes in interpretation and meaning have been identified here and it is important to note that these have occurred not least because of the different *socio-cultural backgrounds* of the performances studied. This factor is particularly relevant because *Swan Lake* is a narrative ballet originally created over a hundred years ago in Russia. The meanings of the Pas de deux, in particular, need to be viewed in relation to certain concepts and conditions prevalent at the time. Meanings in the Pas de deux rely on some understanding of the concept of romantic love between a man and a woman. In the three

Table 9. Chronology of some important productions of *Swan Lake*[1]

Date	Choreographer/Producer/Director/Reviver	Title	First Performance	Reception/Comments
Original Russian Versions				
1877	Reisinger	*Lebedinoe ozero*	Bolshoi Theatre, Moscow	Failure (e.g. Beaumont 1952, Guest 1980)
1880	Hansen	*Lebedinoe ozero*	Bolshoi Theatre, Moscow	
1882	Hansen	*Lebedinoe ozero*	Bolshoi Theatre, Moscow	
1894	Ivanov (Act II only)	*Lebedinoe ozero*	Maryinsky Theatre, St Petersberg	
1895	Petipa & Ivanov (Full ballet)	*Lebedinoe ozero*	Maryinsky Theatre, St Petersberg	Sergeyev participated in the premiére
Productions in England by the Royal Ballet (all after Petipa & Ivanov)				
1932*	Sergeyev & de Valois (Act II only)	*Lac des Cygnes*	London	Markova as Odette/Odile
1934*	Sergeyev revised (full ballet)	*Lac des Cygnes*	Sadler's Wells, London	Markova as Odette/Odile
1936	Sergeyev revised (full ballet)	*Lac des Cygnes*	Sadler's Wells, London	Fonteyn's debut as Odette; Ruth French as Odile
1943	Sergeyev revised (full ballet) (revised version)	*Lac des Cygnes*	Sadler's Wells, London	To mark Sergeyev's departure from SW
1948	Sergeyev revised (i.e. 1934 version revised 1943)	*Lac des Cygnes*	Metropolitan Opera House, New York	1st perf. of co. in US; audiences v. impressed with full-length version – used only to seeing Act II (Bland 1981)
1950	Sergeyev revised (i.e. 1934 version revised 1943)	*Lac des Cygnes*	Metropolitan Opera House, New York	Fonteyn & Somes danced leads
1952*	Ashton & Sergeyev	*Lac des Cygnes*	Royal Opera House, Covent Garden	
1954	Ashton & Sergeyev	*Lac des Cygnes*	Metropolitan Opera House, New York	Not universally liked but Fonteyn & Somes praised for their performances (Bland 1981)

		Lac des Cygnes	**Czinner film** at Royal Opera House, Covent Garden	**Fonteyn & Somes danced leads**
1959	Ashton & Sergeyev	*Swan Lake*	Royal Opera Houe, Covent Garden	
1963*	Added choreography by Ashton, Nureyev & Fay (new revival), directed by Helpmann	*Swan Lake*	Royal Opera House, Covent Garden	Ivanov's choreography for last Act dropped and replaced by Ashton. Interesting rather than successful (Bland 1981)
1971*	Added chor. by Ashton; de Valois; Nureyev; Bruhn Prodn. Sergeyev revised by de Valois	*Swan Lake*	Royal Opera House, Covent Garden	Mixture of 1952 & 1963 versions – found little favour (Bland 1981)
1972	Added chor. by Ashton; de Valois; Nureyev; Bruhn Prodn. Sergeyev revised by de Valois	*Swan Lake*	Royal Opera House, Covent Garden	Makarova made her debut for the Royal Ballet
1972	Supervised by MacMillan (new revival)	*Swan Lake*	Royal Opera House, Covent Garden	Recognised criticism of 1971 version and reverted almost completely to 1952 version. Much preferred (Bland 1981)
1975	Supervised by MacMillan (new revival)	*Swan Lake*	Big Top Tent, London	Makarova & Dowell danced leads
1979*	Slightly modified & renovated version. Added chor. by Ashton; de Valois; Nureyev Prodn. Morrice after Sergeyev	*Swan Lake*	Royal Opera House, Covent Garden	Fairly close to 1952 prodn. but with Ashton chor. for last act from 1963 prodn.
1980	Morrice directed. Chor. by Ashton & Nureyev. Supervised by Ashton, Somes & Gregory	*Swan Lake*	**Thames TV Production** at Royal Opera House, Covent Garden	**Makarova & Dowell danced leads**

1. The Table shows the original Russian versions and productions in England by the Royal Ballet including the filmed and televised versions used for analysis here. The chronology ends with the 1980 Thames Television version.
   * Indicates a new version

contexts relevant here (Russia in 1895, England in 1959 and 1980) the ballet is regarded as an interpretation of a romantic fairy tale, but even fairy tales have different meanings in different contexts. In Tsarist Russia an aristocratic prince such as Siegfried would have been respected and revered by the audience. Indeed the censors decreed that princes should be portrayed as 'ramparts of virtue' (Swift 1968). In the 1950s in England the wealthy 'Prince Charming' of the fairy tale may have provided a similar desirable hero especially for young girls. However, in England in the 1980s some girls and women question the images of the fairy-tale prince and romantic love and expose them as misleading myths which may be seen to be dangerous and oppressive. This is just one example of a possible change in *meaning* and interpretation arising from the changing socio-cultural background.

Another important factor related not only to the socio-cultural background but also to the *theatre context* of the performances of *Swan Lake* is the audience in each instance. In the Maryinsky Theatre in St Petersburg in 1895 the audience was highly aristocratic; in Covent Garden in 1959 it was also drawn mainly from the upper and middle classes; and the spread in 1980 would probably only be slightly wider. However, the audiences for the Czinner film and the Thames TV video are in some senses unlimited and unknown, introducing a new dimension. In order to analyse fully the different interpretations of *Swan Lake* these factors, evident in the analytic framework as *concepts through which interpretation is made* need to be taken into account.

The analytic framework facilitates an examination of the various components evident in the dance that combine to produce the overall statement of meaning. Some aspects of the complexity of the notion of interpretation have been demonstrated, revealing problems of distinction between the interpretations of directors, choreographers and dancers. Nonetheless the analytic framework aids the precise location of the factors within the dance that do not necessarily appear obvious immediately but which contribute to different interpretations. A minimal evaluation of the different interpretations has been attempted here but the material gathered might provide the stimulus for a more detailed evaluation with the aid of the analytic framework.

CHAPTER 8

A history of a dance: an analysis of *Dark Elegies* from written criticism

by Michael Huxley

Historical details and a synopsis of the ballet
The première (1937)
Changes in critics' interpretations and changes in production (1937–81); the critics' reactions; critics' comparisons of style; distinctive features
Evaluative comparisons of productions
Conclusion

Dark Elegies has the distinction of having been in the repertoire of Ballet Rambert since its first performance, whilst, at the same time, other companies have presented different productions of the dance under the supervision of its choreographer, Antony Tudor. Furthermore, it has remained in the Ballet Rambert repertoire despite that company's change of emphasis in artistic policy from classical to modern dance. Both Ballet Rambert and the Royal Ballet presented the dance during the 1980/81 season in London.

The differences between these productions have been a matter of interest to dance critics. Because their views have been committed to print at certain times, it is possible, through analysis, to outline and clarify such differences and to suggest whether they are a result of changes in performance, choreography or production.

One especial value of critics' work is that by virtue of their profession they make it their business to view many different productions of the same dance. Fernau Hall, for instance, committed his thoughts to print in 1950, three decades before expressing his dislike for the Royal Ballet production in 1981. Not only has he seen *Dark Elegies* many times during its history but he has also written about it. John Percival, who has made a detailed study of Tudor's work (1963), has expressed a concern for and an interest in different productions of the dance. In 1972 he compared Ballet Rambert's version with one that had just been staged for the Dutch National Ballet by Tudor himself (Percival 1972, p.49). He suggests that there were some, but few, 'choreographic differences'; the differences in production may derive from the Dutch dancers' performances; the differences in approach might be due to changes in Tudor's style on the one hand or to the interpretation of the Rambert dancers on the other. Like other critics he suggests that whatever the source these differences remain a matter of continuing interest to those who watch ballet.

If, as Percival suggests, Tudor is seen to have changed his mind then so have the critics. The anonymous review of the first performance of *Dark Elegies* in *The Times* (1937) criticises Tudor, concluding that, because of the power of Mahler's score, 'the ballet fails . . . all these solemn posturings can add nothing to the emotional effect of the music'. In the same year the Sitter Out[1] wrote that *Dark Elegies* was

> not a ballet which will have general appeal, but in spite of this it contains many moments of moving beauty, and as an experiment has definite value.
>
> Sitter Out (1937, p.4)

The fact that the dance has now been in Ballet Rambert's repertoire for forty years belies these initial judgements. Thus, whilst it is possible to compare various productions of the dance through critical writing, it has to be acknowledged that interpretations and evaluations have changed too. Dance analysis is used to distinguish between changes in the critics' views and changes in the dance itself by identifying the basis for these interpretations and evaluations.

The following account gives a factual record of different productions and relevant background information. The première is considered in terms of a contemporary review; critics' writings are examined to identify the basis of interpretation and evaluation of *Dark Elegies* between 1937 and 1981; and the various productions of the dance are discussed with reference to these changes.

---

1. P. J. S. Richardson.

Historical details and a synopsis of the ballet

The first performance of *Dark Elegies* was given by Ballet Rambert in February 1937. The choreographer, Antony Tudor, took a leading role in two of the 'songs' in Act One.

Table 10. Details of the première of *Dark Elegies*

company	Ballet Rambert
date	19th February 1937
theatre	Duchess Theatre, London
choreography	Antony Tudor
music	Gustav Mahler *Kindertotenlieder*
design	Nadia Benois
lighting	Richard Caswell
dancers	*1st dance: Peggy Van Praagh and chorus*
	2nd dance: Maude Lloyd and Antony Tudor
	3rd dance: Walter Gore, John Byron, Antony Tudor and chorus
4th dance:	*Agnes de Mille*
5th dance:	*Hugh Laing and chorus*
*chorus:**	*Patricia Clogstoun, Celia Franca, Ann Gee, Daphne Gow, Beryl Kay*
singer	*Harold Child*

*Programmes for later productions include the male soloist in dances 2 and 5 as part of the chorus, hence the attribution of six dancers.

Shortly after this performance Tudor left Ballet Rambert. He took a number of dancers with him and founded his own companies: firstly, Dance Theatre and then London Ballet. He produced *Dark Elegies* for both companies with principal dancers who had performed at the première, notably Hugh Laing and Peggy Van Praagh. In 1940 he emigrated to America and joined Ballet Theatre, where he again produced *Dark Elegies*, dancing with Laing.

In 1944 Marie Rambert revived *Dark Elegies* for her own company, assisted by Van Praagh (at that time with Sadler's Wells Ballet), who had been in all three of the earlier English productions. Walter Gore was also in the cast.

Table 11. Dancers from the première who appeared in later productions 1937–44

Ballet Rambert	(1937)	Tudor, Gore, Laing, Lloyd, de Mille, Van Praagh
Dance Theatre	(1937)	Tudor, Laing, de Mille, Van Praagh
London Ballet	(1938)	Tudor, Laing, Lloyd, Van Praagh
Ballet Theatre	(1940)	Tudor, Laing
Ballet Rambert	(1944)	Gore

During the next three decades Tudor continued to work for Ballet Theatre (later American Ballet Theatre) and for a number of other companies. *Dark Elegies* remained in the repertoire of Ballet Theatre and was revived in 1960 shortly after the company changed its name. Tudor himself became Associate Director of the company in 1974. In the intervening years he worked for the Royal Swedish Ballet from 1949 to 1950, staged *Dark Elegies* for them in 1961, and spent two years as their Ballet director from 1963 to 1964. His productions for these companies, for the National Ballet of Canada and for the Dutch National Ballet all used new designs. The two earlier revivals for Ballet Theatre and the National Ballet of Canada were credited 'after Benois'.

Dark Elegies has remained in the repertoire of Ballet Rambert; produced by Rambert herself and by various company members, but not by Tudor. The original Benois stage cloth designs were retained until the 1969 production when they were replaced by a plain backcloth. The season that introduced the new, modern Rambert in 1966 included *Dark Elegies* as well as other Tudor Ballets. The 1980 revival was in a programme that included another early Tudor work, *Judgement of Paris*, which he made for London Ballet in 1938 and which Rambert had acquired in 1940. The 1980 production of *Dark Elegies* reinstated the original Benois backcloths and was staged by Sally Gilmour, who had assisted with the 1944 revival.

The 1980 Royal Ballet version was neither a new production nor based on the Rambert ones. It was acquired from the Royal Swedish Ballet, using Svensson's designs. The staging was from a Labanotated score of Tudor's 1961 production for that company.

Table 12. Productions of *Dark Elegies* (1937–80)

Dance Theatre	Playhouse Theatre, Oxford, 16 June 1937 prod. Tudor
London Ballet	Toynbee Hall, London, 12 December 1938 prod. Tudor
Ballet Theatre*	Center Theatre, New York, 24 January 1940 prod. Tudor des. Raymond Sovey after Benois
Ballet Rambert (1)	Mercury Theatre, London, 1944 prod. Marie Rambert, assisted by Van Praagh, Gerd Larsen and Sally Gilmour
National Ballet of Canada	Kingston Community Memorial Centre, Kingston, Ontario, Canada, 15 November 1955 prod. Tudor des. Kay Ambrose after Benois
American Ballet Theatre*	Lincoln Center, New York, June 1960 prod. Tudor

Table 12 – *continued*

Royal Swedish Ballet	Royal Opera House, Stockholm, 6 September 1961 prod. Tudor des. Roland Svensson
Ballet Rambert** (2)	Jeannetta Cochrane Theatre, 5 December 1966
Ballet Rambert (3)	Jeannetta Cochrane Theatre, 10 March 1969 des. produced without Benois backcloth
Dutch National Ballet	Stadsschouwburg, Amsterdam, 25 January 1972 prod. Tudor
Ballet Rambert (4)	New Theatre, Oxford, 21 October 1980 prod. Sally Gilmour, assisted by John Chesworth des. Benois
The Royal Ballet	Covent Garden, London, 27 November 1980 prod. Airi Hynninen, from a Labanotated score of the 1961 production des. Svensson

*Ballet Theatre became American Ballet Theatre in 1957.
**First programme of the reformed Ballet Rambert with its new artistic policy under the Associate Director Norman Morrice.
NB *Dark Elegies* has been in the Ballet Rambert repertoire since 1937. The four productions (1–4) listed above marked either changes in the production or in the company.

The music for the original 1937 production was played by a pianoforte quintet. Later productions, particularly the two 1980 productions, used an orchestra.

The dance, which is in two scenes, follows the structure of Mahler's song cycle *Songs on the Death of Children*. The songs are sung to orchestral accompaniment by a solo baritone sitting downstage. The following note was given in the programme for the 1980 Ballet Rambert production:

> After a disaster, young parents mourn the loss of their children.

The first scene, of bereavement, has five dances to five songs performed in front of a backcloth depicting a seascape.[1]

The first dance is a woman's solo, the second a pas de deux. The dance to the third song is a man's solo with an ensemble[2] of five women and one man. All the dancers wear simple costumes.[3] The women are clad in plain, calf-length dresses with a full skirt. Their hair covered by a simple, unpatterned headscarf tied at the nape of the neck. The men wear shirts, trousers and waistcoats. The fourth

---

1. Except in the 1969 Ballet Rambert production.
2. Cohen (1963) describes the dancers as a 'chorus', Brinson and Crisp (1970) use 'ensemble'. In the 1980 productions Rambert uses 'ensemble' the Royal Ballet 'chorus'.
3. Colours and design aspects vary, see page 157.

song is danced by a solo woman and the scene closes with a dance for the ensemble. The soloists are distinguished from the ensemble by certain characteristics of their movement. The former, for instance, use pointe work and turned-out leg positions, the latter do not.

The second scene, of resignation, opens against a backcloth depicting a landscape. The single dance in the scene is for the full company of soloists and ensemble. At the close the dancers leave the stage, two by two, followed by the singer.

Percival gives an uncomplicated description of the action which reflects the clarity of the dance itself.

> All that actually happens in performance is that a man sits on a low stool at the side of the stage, singing a series of songs that reflect the thoughts of a parent on the death of his children. A number of women and men come on and dance; their movements for the most part solemn, with occasional movements expressive of frenzy, grief, or consolation. Generally some of them sit or stand while one or two dance, but at times all join in. Towards the end, after an agitated round dance, their mood becomes more resigned; the backcloth changes from a stormy view of the coast and village; the dancers walk ritually around the stage in quiet procession and go off, followed by the singer.
>
> Percival (1963, pp.31–2)

The première

It is fortunate that *Dark Elegies* survived the poor critical notice given for its first performance. Had we to rely on the *Times* review for any descriptive sense of the dance we would be ill informed. It is worth quoting it in full to demonstrate what can be discerned from it.

Duchess Theatre: A Mahler Ballet

The Ballet Rambert added a new piece to their repertory at the Duchess Theatre on Friday, under the title of *Dark Elegies*, danced to Mahler's *Kindertotenlieder*. It is difficult to think of a work less appropriate to dancing than this song cycle, with its almost uniformly slow rhythms, its subtle poetry, and its intimate expression of personal

146

grief. Mr Antony Tudor, the choreographer, has taken immense pains to construct a suitable choreography on the lines of what may conveniently be called 'symphonic ballet', to distinguish it both from the classical style and from the romantic story-telling kind. He has contrived the joins between one song and the next and the entrances of new characters on the stage with skill, and, wherever the text gave him a cue, he has mirrored the idea in the movements of the dancers – not always with happy effect.

But the ballet fails, because our interest is centred in the voice of the singer, and all these solemn posturings can add nothing to the emotional effect of the music. To an irreverent eye the spectacle might appear to be that of a very serious dress-reform colony going through its morning exercises. But the voice of Mr Harold Child recalls us from such flights of fancy. He sang the songs to the accompaniment of a pianoforte quintet, with steady tone and a genuine feeling for the shape of the phrases, if without enough variety of vocal colour and a sense of dynamic climax to relieve the undoubted monotony of these beautiful songs. The dancers included Miss Agnes de Mille, who came nearest to creating an emotional effect in her solo, Miss Maude Lloyd, Mr Walter Gore, and Mr Antony Tudor himself. Apart from some confusion in the final number, the ballet was well executed in front of two admirable landscapes designed by Miss Nadia Benois.

Anon. (1937)

The review concentrates largely on the music to the exclusion of an immediately apparent description of the dancing. Indeed, description of the dancers and their movements is restricted to the identification of the 'solo' dance. However, the reviewer does indicate certain formal features in the way relationships between the music and the movements through time are described. The dancing follows the music, which is a 'song cycle'. It has 'uniformly slow rhythms' and the dancers' movements mirror 'the text' of the songs. There is, it appears, a continuity in the dancing which carries the action from one of the discrete songs in the cycle to the next. This is achieved by Tudor's 'skill' in contriving 'joins' with the entrance of new characters.

The reviewer gives a further indication of the form of the dance in interpreting it as 'symphonic' rather than 'classical' or 'romantic'. The term 'symphonic ballet' was used in the 1930s to describe Massine's choreography to symphonic music[1] and this becomes a device to distinguish Tudor's choreography from previous ballet styles and to locate it in a contemporary style associated with a recognised choreographer.

Much of the review is taken up with evaluation. The singer is praised technically for his 'steady tone' and interpretatively for his 'genuine feeling for the shape of the phrases'. He is, however, found wanting in his 'variety of vocal colour' and sense of 'dynamic climax'. The dancers are judged less comprehensively. De Mille's intepretation comes near to 'creating an emotional effect' and the ballet is technically 'well executed' despite 'some confusion in the final number'.

The main comment is on the appropriateness of the choreographic treatment of the music. Although the songs themselves are 'monotonous', they are judged to be beautiful. The dance treatment is found to mirror it, but 'not always with happy effect'. The conclusion is that the treatment is 'inappropriate'. Certain features contribute to this judgement. The subject is identified as the music, not the music's own subject, grief. This leads to an attribution of a 'symphonic' style to the work and an evaluation based on the appropriateness of the choreographic treatment of the music.

The writer is not averse to 'personal grief', but implies that this is not appropriate for dance. The 'emotional' qualities of the music are applauded to the detriment of the choreographic qualities, which do not achieve the same effect. It is the movement with which the reviewer finds fault, with what are regarded as 'solemn posturings' and 'exercises'. These faults are compounded because, in following the music closely, the movements do not effectively enhance its 'uniformly slow rhythms' and 'undoubted monotony'. The dance is therefore seen to add nothing to the music's beauty or meaning.

1. For instance, *Choreatium* to Brahms' 4th Symphony (1933).

Changes in critics' interpretations and changes in production (1937–81)

Critics' reactions

Since the first antipathetic notice in 1937 *Dark Elegies* has received near unanimous praise for its choreography. At the same time such recognition has been acknowledged by many critics to be a retrospective assessment. For instance, in 1980 Goodwin writes:

> what must have seemed a daring use of music at that time (1937) has long been shown to have the essential elements of a choreographic imagination entirely at one with the musical character.
>
> Programme note (1980)

In trying to judge the significance of the dance writers have compared it with classical ballet's twentieth-century tradition. As early as 1938 Coton (1938, p.154) described it as the crowning achievement of a series of choreographic experiments by Ballet Rambert. Later:

> *Dark Elegies* was the first, and remains the greatest, English work of ballet on a serious theme.
>
> Coton (1941–2), p.62)

Hall (1950, p.112) suggests that the critics' reactions to the first performance were due to an inability to come to terms with the way *Dark Elegies* 'went so far beyond existing conceptions of the proper scope of a ballet'. However,

> in England, the public gradually became used to the idiom of *Dark Elegies*, and as the strangeness wore off its greatness has been more and more widely recognised.
>
> Hall (1950, p.112)

Many writers make favourable comparisons with *Dark Elegies'* antecedents. Coton compares it directly with the work of Fokine and Massine.

> One of the first indices of an awareness of the existence of this path (amongst choreographers) was the creation of this work.
>
> Coton (1938, p.154)

149

Twenty-five years later Percival considers how much *Dark Elegies* owed to the influence of these choreographers and to the styles established in *Les Sylphides* and *Les Presages*. He concludes:

> that no one before Tudor had tried to produce a ballet like *Dark Elegies*, that few have tried in the quarter century since *Elegies* was first given, and that none succeeded.
>
> Percival (1963, p.31)

Similar praise is evident in Goodwin's consideration of attempts to follow Tudor's lead in the use of Mahler's music where he judges *Dark Elegies* to be a 'classic of its genre'. (1980).

Many reasons have been offered for these and similar judgements. They appear to fall into two quite distinct categories. Firstly, they attempt to place *Dark Elegies* by making comparisons with other dance styles. Secondly, they attempt to characterise the distinctive features of the ballet itself.

Critics' comparisons of style

In the original *Times* review (1937) it was thought expedient to distinguish the new work as a 'symphonic ballet' in order to differentiate it from earlier classical and romantic styles. Later writers attempt comparisons with other artistic and choreographic styles. Coton (1938), Brinson and Van Praagh (1963) and Percival (1963) compare Tudor's choreographic style with that of Fokine; Brinson and Van Praagh suggest a further comparison with Jooss. Brinson and Crisp (1970) identify 'expressionism' as an influence, while Lloyd (1949) places the work within 'modernism' but with some reservations.

Although Percival is eager to praise the ballet's stylistic antecedents he also suggests that the differences between them are to be found in

> all the constituent parts of *Dark Elegies*, in the choice of theme, music and designs and in the choreography as a whole.
>
> Percival (1963, p.34)

In terms of analysis this refers to movement, aural and visual components; form; subject matter; treatment and the effectiveness of the choreography. Taken together, they can be used to characterise the style of the work and its significance.

With this range of characteristics in mind it is possible to look again at writers' comparisons with other styles. The *Times* (1937) reviewer's description, 'symphonic ballet', is used to distinguish it from the 'romantic story-telling kind', while Coton (1958, p.153), in drawing the comparison more specifically with Fokine's style, identifies the 'lack of story content' as a major feature. It is this aspect of Fokine's choreograpic style that leads Percival (1963, p.31) to compare *Dark Elegies* with *Les Sylphides*, where Fokine made 'a [plotless] series of dances that hang together as a complete whole'. In *Dark Elegies*

> Tudor saw, as others had done, that Les Sylphides was the first ballet that set out, without any plot, to evoke a mood.
>
> Percival (1963, p.31)

Brinson and Van Praagh's account of Fokine's influence makes a similar comparison (1963, p.87).

The 1937 evaluations stress 'mood'. The *Times* (1937) review criticises the choreography of *Dark Elegies* for not matching the music's 'intimate expression of personal grief' and singles out de Mille, who 'came nearest to creating an emotional effect'. The Sitter Out (1937, p.4) conceded that Tudor is successful 'on the whole' . . . in conveying an atmosphere charged with restrained emotion'.

The specific historical location of the dance becomes important when an 'expressionist' or 'Central European' stylistic influence is identified. By 1937 the 'Central European' style of early modern dance had been popularised in England by Ballets Jooss among others.

Brinson and Crisp(1970, p.143)[1] go so far as to say that the 'principal stylistic influence is expressionist'. The point is made more specifically by Brinson and Van Praagh (1963, p.87) when they identify an 'influence' as the 'expressionist work of Kurt Jooss'. Both these remarks about style were made some time after the ballet's première and it may be that they attempt to identify the period rather than specific features of the dance. On the other hand

---

1. Brinson and Crisp's assessments of *Dark Elegies* were first made in *Ballet for all* (1970 and reiterated in their later (1980) book.

Coton (1941–2) wrote during the period itself and was responsible for a biography of Jooss (1946). In considering *Dark Elegies* he is quite precise about where the Central European influence might be seen.

> In the individual dances for the different men and women Tudor . . . has matched the classical neatness of turn and expressiveness of carriage with the freer plastic gestures, drawn from the Central European style of movement.
>
> Coton (1941–2, p.62)

This identification of a Central European influence in some of the movements may explain some of the *Times* reviewer's antipathy.

The Central European style and Expressionism were both modern movements. In characterising *Dark Elegies* as 'near the modern idiom' Lloyd (1949, p.328), is careful to suggest that the 'movements derived from no [particular] school of modernism', rather, the comparison refers to the treatment of the subject of emotion. She finds it a very difficult dance to characterise stylistically and identifies its differences in form from the ballet and modern dance styles of the time.

> According to American modern standards, the formal patterns are too symmetrical . . . the rhythms are not sufficiently harsh. According to the strict ballet standards it does not quite belong.
>
> Lloyd (1949, p.328)

Denby, also writing from an American viewpoint, suggests that the ritual forms in the dance date it.

> They look a little like modern dancers of some years back doing a symbolic number.
>
> Denby (1944, p.74)

To summarise, writers have used comparisons with other styles to identify the characteristic mood (quality) of the subject of *Dark Elegies*, grief. Where style has been used to characterise the actual components of the ballet the references tend to be certain movement components and formal features and not to the choreography as a whole. The other features mentioned by Percival have not been used in these comparisons and are now considered.

Distinctive features

Coton's identification of Central European dance movements is only part of his description.

> This union of styles is freely leavened with adaptions from steps, gestures, head movements he had watched for in the everyday life of the street.
>
> Coton (1941–2, p.62)

Hall suggests that

> Tudor does not use a single pure [ballet] classroom step in the whole length of *Dark Elegies*.
>
> (1950, p.115)

and that there is evidence to suggest that the ballet's 'roots' also derive from 'folk dance'. This genre is used in a specific part of the ballet, 'particularly in its mass dances' (Hall 1950, p.112)

Various interpretations of the use of components from these different styles and genres are given. For instance, Brinson and Van Praagh suggest:

> the steps are still the steps of the danse d'école but they are moulded in new ways and combined with new movements for emotional effect.
>
> Brinson and Van Praagh (1963, p.184)

Other writers also note how the use of these different steps and the way they are placed in relation to each other create particular formal features which contribute to the mood. Hall suggests that, despite the apparent contradiction of having 'simple peasant women' dancing 'en pointe', this use is appropriate in creating a mood of austerity. The pertinence is to be found in the formal arrangement of the steps which creates a subtle relation between the moment and the linear development to produce repeated accents. Tudor introduces

> poses on pointe from time to time as a natural culmination to certain phrases, without the slightest break in texture.
>
> Hall (1950, p.113)

This use is made clearer by Brinson and Crisp's observation that pointe is only used by the three principals, thereby forming another relation between the dancers' movements which makes use of these differences. The result provides

> a contrast which helps to emphasise choreographically
> the sense of grief and personal loss.
>
> Brinson and Crisp (1970, p.143)

Here the precise way in which the choreography treats the subject to create the qualities of the dance is described in terms of a specific relation.

Coton and other writers remark on the use of steps and gestures taken from everyday life. At first this would appear to contradict critics' interpretation of *Dark Elegies* as a non-literal, plotless 'ballet' that does not tell a story. However, Percival explains how such gestures are not given a literal relation through time.

> Now and again in *Dark Elegies* comes a gesture that is recognisably taken from life – as when the man in the duet to the second song places his hand on the shoulder of the woman to comfort her. Such incidents are rare, however, and do not form part of a logical narrative.
>
> Percival (1963, p.33)

It is not the specific gestures which are used to convey grief but the way such gestures and the other various steps are arranged in relation to each other.

> Most of the movement in *Dark Elegies* carries no specific connotation of grief, despair, or any other emotion. It makes its point through the way it is organised as a whole.
>
> (*ibid*).

Hall, in describing the overall structure, pays attention to the way each dance relates to the whole and attributes the building of atmosphere and mood to its linear development.

> Each solo dance emerges smoothly and naturally from a mass dance of the chorus, and merges back into the mass at the end. The ballet rises to a stern climax in the storm scene with its liberation of pent-up emotions, and then the tension gradually relaxes to a note of resignation, with the dancers leaving the stage two by two.
>
> Hall (1950, p.113)

The emphasis on form in the treatment of the subject is not fortuitous. Percival points out that

> this is, in the classical definition, a rising tragedy – the catastrophe comes first, to be followed by acceptance and a quiet ending.
>
> Percival (1963, p.34)

Moreover, he suggests that it is this treatment that not only distinguishes *Dark Elegies* from other dances on a similar theme but also accounts for its superiority.

> *Dark Elegies* differs from the many ballets that have an unhappy ending but lack the essential ingredients of tragedy . . . [It] is tragic in the full sense: it is noble; it moves with inevitable logic.
>
> (*ibid*).

With the exception of the 1937 reviews of the dance most critics have acclaimed it both as remarkable for its time and as an enduring work. Central to all their evaluations is the quality that the dance creates. The distinctive features of *Dark Elegies*' components are applauded, not for their novelty, but for the way they contribute formally to an appropriate choreographic treatment of its subject. The subject of the dance is identified as the way all these distinctive features contribute to its unique statement about tragedy.

Evaluative comparisons of productions

All the writings quoted attempt to interpret and evaluate *Dark Elegies* although very few contain specific references to the production on which their authors' assessments are made.

Coton's (1938) writing refers to the Ballet Rambert original. His later (1941–2) article is about London Ballet but his comments on *Dark Elegies* are based on the February 1937 Rambert season. Hall's (1950) work refers specifically to the première but also, by implication to Tudor's other English productions for Dance Theatre and London Ballet. Percival (1963) does not directly refer to any one production. His article is specifically concerned with Tudor's 'years in England' and the illustrations are from the 1937 production. He also notes that 'one can watch it as often as the infrequent opportunity arises, finding new satisfaction at every repetiton' (Percival 1963, p.33). Brinson and Van Praagh do not cite a specific production but the latter danced in both 1937 productions, in the 1938 one, and helped stage the 1944 revival.

Two of these writers, Hall and Percival, make subsidiary reference to productions other than the original, remarking on performance style and sets.

> Those who never saw one of Tudor's English productions of this ballet can only get a faint idea of its grandeur from the Rambert revival [1944]; in fact, Tudor himself had a very limited success when he attempted to produce the ballet in New York with American dancers unfamiliar with his style.
>
> Hall (1959, p.113)

Both the Dance Theatre and London Ballet productions used dancers from the original season. Hall quite clearly identifies the performance style of the American dancers as a reason for their less successful interpretation. The reasons for Ballet Rambert's lack of grandeur are not given.

Percival suggests that despite Benois' successful sets it was her costume designs that greatly helped 'create the mood' because 'the dancers look like real people'. In 1963, shortly after revivals by American Ballet Theatre and the Royal Swedish Ballet (designed by Svensson), he notes that

> in some recent revivals the men's clothes have changed, becoming more fanciful and less realistic, and the ballet suffers.
>
> Percival (1963, p.34)

Later writers extend their criticisms to the sets as well. Dodd (1969) is 'shocked' by the 1969 Ballet Rambert production that dispensed with Benois' painted backcloth. Clarke (1981a) looks favourably on the Svensson designs for the Royal Ballet production.

It has been noted that *Dark Elegies* is distinguished historically by its many productions and these have been identified in Table 12 with reference to different producers and designers. Analysis enables us to discern what effect these changes have had and to what extent they have contributed to the value of a production. The following account discusses evaluations of design and performance.

Percival's (1963) criticism of design changes centres on the costumes rather than the set. His later review of the Dutch National Ballet production criticises the change of colour of the costumes. Here the dark red and blue of the women's dresses are replaced by a 'paler blue and a nasty mauve' (1972, p.50). However, he finds the set design – a blue backcloth 'with just a groundrow of rocks in the front' – to be appropriate.

Clarke (1981a, p.238), in comparing the 1980 British productions, identifies Ballet Rambert's Benois sets as one reason for the production's superiority over the Royal Ballet version, the latter's designs, by Svensson, being a 'pallid representation and undistinguished'. Hall, comparing the same productions, identifies the Benois set as one feature contributing to the superior 'general atmosphere' of the Rambert version because of the relation between design and the formal structures of the ensemble work.

> the patterns of the group dancing . . . were wonderfully attuned to the Benois setting
>
> Hall (1981)

The most strident criticism of the set of a new production is to be found in Dodd's review of the 1969 Ballet Rambert production with its decorless setting.[1] He explains the effect this had.

> The work appears to have lost a dimension and to have become less personal and real. It now looks like a dozen other modern ballets
>
> Dodd (1969, p.408)

This is an interesting point because the earlier analysis of the ballet identified its differences from other styles as a characteristic and important feature. The next Ballet Rambert production in 1980 reinstated the backcloths and was praised accordingly.

Hall's (1950) comparison between performances of the original three English productions, the first Rambert revival and the first Ballet Theatre production, identifies the dancers' performance as a reason for their significant differences. Later writers have commented on more recent productions and have emphasised dancers'

---

1. Percival (1972, p.49) suggests that Tudor had, at one time, considered using a plain black backcloth but had not put the idea into practice.

157

interpretations of mood. Clarke comments on the 1967 Ballet Rambert production:

> Christopher Gable... gave the impression of being really stunned, drenched in grief.
>
> Clarke (1967, p.178)

Dodd considers the next, 1969, production.

> A more mechanical way of dancing instead of acting it...weakens the emotional effect.
>
> Dodd, (1969, p.408)

Percival compares the Rambert production with that of the Dutch National Ballet, who achieve:

> a much less heavy effect, less sense of being weighed down with grief.
>
> Percival (1972, p.49)

The most direct comparison is made in support of judgements on the relative merits of the 1980/81 Ballet Rambert and Royal Ballet productions. Both Clarke and Hall prefer the Rambert version. Hall suggesting that:

> the dancers showed the right qualities of understatement and devotional intensity.
>
> Hall (1981)

Clarke suggests that the Royal Ballet version

> lacks the emotion of shared grief that was once so strong.
>
> Clarke (1981a, p.238)

She identifies the differences of quality in particular dynamic elements of the dancers' interpretation.

> The Royal Ballet dancers are basically too light-weight and classical in their approach. With Tudor, the movement in a modern work is down.
>
> (*ibid.*)

Dromgoole (1981) is more concerned with comparing the 1981 Rambert version with the original in 1937, 'when things were otherwise'. His complaint is that for 'contemporary' performers 'emotion, any kind of emotion is almost a dirty word'. Thus, although the dancers 'did the movements competently enough', they were found to be wanting in 'expressing anguish and grief'.

All these reviews are concerned with comparisons that emphasise companies' interpretations. The differences in the actual choreography are rarely touched on but, when they are, the question of the version rather than the correct interpretation is raised. Percival, reviewing the Dutch National Ballet notices:

> only in one dance was I conscious of much choreographic difference from the version preserved by Ballet Rambert- ...This difference was in the male sole of the third song . . .which seemed to have more detail.
>
> Percival (1972, p.49)

Hall, who had seen the original 1937 production, faults both the 1980 productions.

> The choreography of the Rambert version, showed a good many faults – the first dance image performed by the first soloist as she came on stage, for example, included a swooping lunge which was quite wrong – but the Royal Ballet's version, uncorrected by Tudor, also had numerous flaws.
>
> Hall (1981)

In both cases the 'differences' in choreography appear to be restricted to a few movements and such changes will alter the formal relations deriving from them but none of the critics suggest that these relations or the overall structure have changed significantly.

Conclusion

The critics who have commented on *Dark Elegies* during its long and diverse history appear to have offered many reasons for the success of its choreography and the relative values of different productions. This analysis has shown that certain features of the ballet have been regarded as more important then others.

Those writers who have attempted to interpret and evaluate the choreography have emphasised the plotless treatment of grief which concentrates on the creation of moods and atmosphere to convey the meaning of the tragedy. Despite the use of movement components drawn from different styles and genres the mood is established by their formal relations rather than by any literal meaning attached to the movements themselves. It is these relations, especially those through time, which are unique and which establish the treatment of the subject. Writers have commented on choreographic changes from production to production although these seem to be of movement components and not significant relations in the form of the dance.

All early reviews of the work, including the unfavourable ones, refer to its particular mood and this is stressed in later evaluations. Changes in quality are seen to arise largely from different dancers' (and companies') interpretations in performance. Where there is a failure to re-create the qualities of the original work two reasons may be cited. Firstly, that the dancers are not sufficiently conversant with Tudor's late 1930s style or are used to dances with very different dynamic elements, Secondly, where Tudor has been producer, the qualities of the ballet and the interpretation have been changed by the choreographer himself.

Tudor may have changed the emphasis of the ballet's qualities but the treatment appears to have remained the same except in one respect, its design. Although early critics applaud Benois' set and costume designs no great emphasis is placed on their contribution to the work as a whole. However, when these designs have been replaced they have been remarked on. The designs for Tudor's later productions seem to have changed in emphasis rather than content. The importance of a painted backcloth in establishing the ballet's style is emphasised when the decor-less 1969 production is considered.

Most critics place considerable emphasis on the importance of *Dark Elegies* as a dance of its time. Much of their writing harks back to the first performances as a reference point. It is not surprising that the 1980 Rambert revival, with its original Benois designs, meets with approval. What is interesting is that the style of that period and the mood of intense emotion are regarded as appropriate and important contributions to a company's 1980/81 season. Writers in the 1930s and 1940s were hard-pressed to define the dance accurately or comprehensively in terms of others' styles but were convinced of its uniqueness. This may well account for *Dark Elegies'* subsequent success in its many productions as part of both classical and modern repertoires.

CHAPTER 9

Approaches to new dance: an analysis of two works

Are You Right There Michael Are You Right?: Fergus Early
  by Michael Huxley
Manipulatin' motion (pictures): Laurie Booth
  by Valerie A Briginshaw
Approaches to new dance
  by Valerie A Briginshaw and Michael Huxley

The experimental and avant garde nature of new dance[1] expands the boundaries of what is recognised and accepted as dance. Clearly this poses problems in appreciation and critics have been taken to task for employing inappropriate criteria when writing about it, especially by *New Dance* magazine:

> The critics appear to speak from the middle ground of dance thinking in Britain and this position is based on aesthetic and social assumptions which are quite different to [those of] New Dance.... If the work must be categorised in order to be considered then it will remain truly invisible.
>
> Crickmay (1982,pp.7–8)

Performances of new dance can be very different from those of other dance theatre genres and styles and sometimes the difference is so great that critics question the appropriateness of using the term 'dance' at all, for instance Woodward (1981, p.41) on Moulton's *Nine Person Precision Ball Passing.*

---

1. The term 'new dance' has become common currency since *New Dance* magazine was first published in 1977. Both Early and Booth have been involved with the magazine: Early as a member of the editorial collective. Booth has contributed, and, like Early, has had his work reviewed in it.

Our concern is not to enter a debate about what is dance but rather, when something is presented as dance, to examine and analyse it using an appropriate framework. In this chapter we analyse two examples of new dance and discuss the problems that may be encountered. Particular attention is given to the treatment of subject matter in Early's work and to the problems of evaluation in Booth's.

Are You Right There Michael Are You Right? (1982)
Choreography and performance: Fergus Early
Design: Gregory Smith

Fergus Early's 'solo dance theatre show' is a two-act work about his father, Noel Early. The title is taken from a song by Percy French which is used in the performance.

The story begins in Ireland, where Noel Early was born and brought up. The location is set by upstage projections of the Irish countryside, followed by two Irish dance tunes which introduce Fergus Early's first dance, which borrows patterns from Irish folk dances. Its youthful vitality comes both from these steps and from the additional jumps and steps that fill the stage. The story progresses visually through a number of scenes. Slide projections and changes of decor depict Ireland, India, England and Korea; ending in a rather nondescript fifties sitting room in England.

Early, portraying his father, 'inhabits' these scenes, changing costume so that in each scene he is dressed appropriately for the period: tropical kit with shorts and sola topi in India, dark suit in England. The performer spends much time creating tableaux and images. Often he does nothing more than sit in a chair – a canvas one in India, an armchair in England.

Occasionally in each scene he breaks into a short dance, which is recognised as part of the period through the accompanying music and costume. There is no attempt to re-create dances of the period in toto. Their steps and stepping patterns (as in the initial jig) are blended with low jetés and attenuated arabesques and this use of recognisable components of the ballet vocabularly is characteristic of the performance as a whole.

The story proceeds chronologically through Act One, tracing Noel Early's life in the Indian Medical Service, his return to England in 1947 and his subsequent involvement in the Korean war, where an accident disables him. In Act Two, again in England, there are occasional 'flashbacks' where sections of songs used earlier, such as the title tune, and brief dance phrases, recall previous scenes.

Are You Right There Michael Are You Right? (hereafter referred to as *Michael*) is an extremely complex and highly structured work of dance theatre. Each component is accorded an equal importance in telling the story but attention is constantly drawn from one to the other – from slides to a new costume to a short dance and then back again to the soundtrack

Despite the use of steps from different styles and genres the overall range of movement is not great and it is executed within a modest spatial and dynamic range. Jumps and turns appear close to the body because their lines are never extended to the full. The faster dances of Act One make much use of quick, neat steps: the slower ones use attenuated positions with soft arms and an unextended body, giving them a curved rather than linear quality. In Act Two falls and locomotion are employed in a dance where the performer, 'injured' and using his crutch, falls to the floor.

The visual setting is important, the dancer using numerous props and costumes. During Act One he dances with larger than life size models representing other characters, and with an unseen partner. These models inhabit the set in much the same way as the performer does, somewhat passively, becoming part of the scene, moved from place to place. The visual environment is constantly changed. Two large screens, when turned to face the audience, become rooms in character with the clothes they contain. Other pieces of scenery, such as a working two-dimensional cartoon of Early's family, are brought on and manipulated by the dancer. An entire section involves the dancer simply and carefully laying out small Indian rugs to cover the stage.

A most noticeable and enduring feature of the performance is the taped accompaniment. The few short songs which accompany most of the dances are interludes in a complex spoken narrative of taped reminscences by (Fergus) Early's mother, two sisters, a brother and an uncle. Each family member recalls their own impressions of Noel Early at different times in his life. These stories are told quietly and often at length during the performance, frequently constituting the only action in the theatre. Throughout the performance the audience never has to listen to more than one thing at a time. The recollections weave a web in the story that they tell. The dancer himself never speaks.

The complexes formed from these components and elements are highly selective. The Irish dance is performed in front of a view of Ireland accompanied by an Irish dance tune. One of the Indian scenes finds Early sitting, upstage centre, in front of a photograph (back-projected) of his father. He is dressed in a similar costume and sits quite still while taped reminiscences detail his experiences in that country. There is never any attempt to baffle the senses by using all the available components at one time. Neither is there any attempt to present events synchronously. Each is taken in turn. The movements, the set, costumes and photographs, the songs and the recorded voices are brought together sparingly to produce a series of extended images, sometimes retaining the image long enough for it to form a section of the scene.

These sections are characteristic of the form of the dance. They tend to be discrete but their linear relationships depend on the way one section or one scene changes to another. These changes are executed on stage by the performer. He manipulates the props, brings scenery on stage and changes costume many times in front of the audience. This procedure both demystifies the theatrical process and gives a visual continuity which would otherwise be interrupted by blackouts.

The developing story does not retrace its steps visually. However, some of the movements are repeated from dance to dance, especially the positions and jumps taken from ballet. The main linear development is supplied by the voices on the soundtrack, which continue during the different types of stage action: while the meticulously executed costume changes take place; while Early sits or walks about the stage; while the projections and scene changes indicate the passing of time. The images within each scene continue the narrative, each one being different. Some are quite long but restrict movement to functional action such as the changing from an army uniform with jacket, trousers and belt to tropical kit. Others are momentary – the change from a photograph of Noel Early to one which sets the context of colonial India. The 'danced' images are highlighted by their own components. With so much subdued functional action each of the dances appears as a wealth of movement, separating it from the mundane. The difference, and emphasis, is further provided by the greater dynamic range and spatial use that the dances employ. Each image has a different duration, all but one of the dances is accompanied by short folk tunes or popular songs of similar length,[1] thereby distinguishing them from other images.

Styles, and particularly choreographers' styles, become distinguishable from other styles by the development and use of a particular vocabulary. To some small extent this is true of Early and his work.The attenuated spatial lines and some of the positions developed from the ballet vocabulary that are evident in *Michael* can also be seen in much of his other work. Similarly, he has a distinctive performance style, a somewhat diffident presentation which belies the expected macho role of the male dancer. This is noticeable in both *I, Giselle* (1981) and the earlier *Sunrise* (1979). However, in both *I, Giselle* (choreographed jointly with Jacky Lansley) and *Michael* the choreographic distinctiveness is largely in the self-effacing use of dynamic and spatial elements and not in the choice and combination of movements. Indeed, as has been noted, many steps are borrowed from established genres. These are not presented as complete dances within the style from which they arise; neither is any attempt made to disguise them by developing them into a distinctive Early vocabulary. The steps retain their own identity.

In addition to occasional ballet movements the dance has other features usually associated with the Romantic Ballet: the type of subject chosen and its treatment. *Michael* takes a story which Early treats as a narrative in a linear, chronological account, using a number of discrete scenes to move the action from place to place. The details of the story are conveyed largely through means other than dancing while the dances serve to highlight emotional states of the central character. Costume and set are vital in placing the action. In contrast the use of modern theatrical techniques, particularly back-projected slides, is characteristic of (although not exclusive to) modern dance. Yet *Michael* differs markedly from both ballet and modern dance in a number of crucial respects:

the personal nature of the subject matter
the deliberate juxtaposition of styles
the formal presentation

---

1. The length of a '78' record.

the equal status afforded dance, functional movement and sections with no stage action at all

the use of a realistic soundtrack account of the subject.

It is these features which, taken together, direct the audience's attention to the subject of the performance, to the story itself. Early uses an established subject, a story, treats it in a narrative manner as in ballet and presents it in a modern theatrical context. In doing so he disrupts certain values of the genres and styles from which he draws.

This disruption through reinterpretation of established values is explicit in his earlier work with Lansley, *I, Giselle*. They comment:

> a lot of new dance has rejected everything associated with classical ballet, but we both have a background in ballet and we want to reclaim some of its positive elements and skills, particularly its theatrical quality, and use these in new contexts.
>
> Programme note (1981)

I, Giselle takes an established story and examines 'its politics, its ideology, its sexual roles' (*ibid*). *Michael* shows the same concern for the ballet vocabulary and for its theatricality. But whereas in *I, Giselle* these 'skills' are used to reinterpret an existing story, in *Michael* a previously unknown story is told.

In a programme note Early gives brief biographical details about his father: Irish, a doctor who worked in the Indian army. After a brief period in England following India's independence he went back into action in Korea, where he was injured in a jeep accident. On returning to England he began to drink heavily, became ill and died of cancer. Such details, known before the action begins, provide some of the concepts through which the work is interpreted. We also know that Fergus was eight when his father died and this is biography, not recollection.

The story has much in common with many literary and theatrical themes: working and marrying in a distant land with a wholly different culture; disillusionment; disablement; a decline in another foreign country (England) helped by alcohol and ending in a premature death. What distinguishes it is that the story is told as dance by the subject's son. Biographical subjects are quite common in both modern dance and ballet; for instance in Martha Graham's *Letter to the World* (1940) about Emily Dickinson, and in Ashton's

Enigma Variations (1968) on the life of Edward Elgar. Death is the subject of a number of dances; for instance Tudor's *Dark Elegies* (1937), which considers grieving after death, and North's *Death and the Maiden* concerned with impending death.

Early's treatment differs markedly from these stylised accounts in the way he has chosen not to distance himself from his father's life and death. Rather than use a symbolic form which abstracts emotion he has chosen to present the story as a direct, linear narrative and, furthermore, to dance the role of his father himself. What is remarkable is that such a subject and its treatment do not lead to an indulgence in the emotionalism inherent in such a subject. It is this that serves as a contradistinction from the Romantic death and from the emotive rendering of personal feelings evident in some modern dance. The investigation of one's father's life, decline and death must have involved intense emotion but the choreography and theatrical presentation use certain formal devices that effectively distance him from the subject and its treatment.

One particular instance in the dance, a moment that stands out in time, illustrates this. It becomes apparent early on that Fergus bears a close physical resemblance to his father, Noel. At the time of the first performance he was thirty-five years old. Many of the projected photographs of Noel Early are directly imitated on stage in Fergus's use of similar costume. No attempt is made, however, to suggest ageing through theatrical artifice. During one of the Indian scenes, when Noel must have been in his thirties, Fergus sits upstage in front of a projected picture of his father. The clothing, chair and posture contrive to be similar and the visible resemblance between the two is quite remarkable. The close relationship between father and son, subject and performer, is never more strikingly made. However, the reference is a subdued one. The action directly prior to the pose makes no hint of an impending visual climax. Nothing, other than the position and the photograph, is used to emphasise the point. Indeed, at this time attention is focussed on the spoken reminiscences. The image is presented as one theatrical point among many.

The use and juxtaposition of other components also serves to distance the performer from his subject. For instance, the other characters, when introduced, are all non-realistic models. The family group in Ireland is a near life size cut out model with moving legs, which Early dances with, kicking it into action. The almost surreal images are set against either popular songs or the realistic narrative. The difference is also seen as the work proceeds: the cartoon family contrasting strongly with the realism of the performer portraying his father whilst listening to his family's account of his life.

The effect is to disrupt and disturb the linear quality of the story and the spoken account. The reminiscences and the place, as described in the geographical scenes, have a recognisable continuity. However, the different treatments and the constantly changing viewpoint of the narrative (brother, mother, sister, uncle) serve to question rather than reinforce the inevitability of the story that is expected: the family account appears more in sympathy with some periods than others. Although the contradictions in style and components do not in themselves directly emphasise contradictions in the story, their effect, in a Brechtian sense, constantly draws attention back to it, exposing the way in which it is being told, reminding us who is telling it on stage.

In both *Michael* and *I, Giselle* Early considers certain values associated with the period of the story and with its treatment in the 1980s. In *I, Giselle* Albrecht is trapped by the Romantic role accorded him, in a version where Giselle discovers his subterfuge in Act One, and he is punished for his deception rather than his noble love. In *Michael* Noel Early is made neither hero nor victim; rather, he appears to be trapped in the culture of colonial India. He dons its attributes like costumes without which, in Act Two, he becomes increasingly vulnerable.

The treatment both questions and contradicts some of the values inherent in the styles from which Early borrows. In *I, Giselle* he dances Albrecht in a way which exposes the character's vulnerability. In *Michael* he has chosen a subject which, by its personal nature, makes him vulnerable as both choreographer and performer. Rather than succumb to this vulnerability he incorporates it, as his view of his father, into the subject matter. That is to say that the subject becomes Fergus Early's view of his father's story. In this way his viewpoint becomes subject rather than treatment and the treatment itself uses certain formal devices to distance the performer from the subject. The dancer therefore retains the security of the theatre performer while being able to question the attitudes that make this distancing necessary – attitudes about what is acceptable as a man's social role.

The questioning of men's roles[1] whilst not unique to new dance is readily accommodated by and characteristic of it. In *Michael* the usual subjects for a male dance role and a solo man's dance performance are also questioned, particularly those concerned with close familial relationships. Such a subject is not a usual topic of male conversation except in times of stress. Early's work challenges such assumptions and, in doing so, the presumption that men in an audience cannot be publicly moved by such topics.

Although Early may be said to have a certain choreographic and performance style, such characterisation cannot be made in the strong sense of the terms. Neither is it possible to place his work conclusively within a recognised style or genre by an analysis based on movement and form alone. However, there are a number of distinctive features of *Michael* which reflect the characteristic and underlying values of new dance:

the use of seemingly disparate movement components from a number of existing styles

the deliberate inversion and contradiction of formal features with an accepted style and treatment

the deliberate conjunction of distinct and opposing stylistic devices

the choice of a personal subject matter not usually found in dance

the treatment of subject matter which, by disrupting notions of style, questions values implicit in that style.

Taken together these features direct the viewer's attention to the meaning in the subject. Again, a key feature of new dance.

No attempt has been made to deal with an evaluation of this work. However, it is obvious that any assessment must take into account these features. It would be inappropriate to judge it by the values of any of the contributory genres and styles because of the way in which they are used. Equally, in that the subject is of central importance, evaluation is concerned not only with how this is used as a subject for dance but also with the subject itself. It is in this sense that further conventional values are questioned. In *Are You Right There Michael Are You Right?* Fergus Early is exposing his father's life, his own feelings towards his father and the whole purpose of male dance to public scrutiny and judgement.

---

1. Equally, many solo women's new dance performances question the conventional views of a woman's role.

Manipulatin' Motion (Pictures) (1981)
Choreography and performance: Laurie Booth

As the audience enters the theatre[1] Booth is shuffling across the space; he turns and shuffles back, turns and moves away from and towards the audience, all of this performed quite slowly. The atmosphere is concentrated, quiet and purposeful, the only sound is the regular rhythm of Booth's shuffling, slippered feet. He stops, facing the audience and looks for a moment, as he continues he raises his feet from the ground and the accompaniment disappears. His travelling gets slightly faster and the movements a little bigger as his feet come further off the ground and his legs make small circling gestures in the air retaining the fluidity of his former T'ai Chi-like style. The silence is broken and Booth states:

> it is a commonly known fact that many immigrants made their fortunes in the new world and in their old age they return to the towns, hamlets, villages of their origins amidst memories of adventure, images of youth.

He talks in this half-lecturing, half-poetic style sometimes addressing the audience while standing still, sometimes while he is dancing.

The dance lasts for about one hour. Booth accompanies it variously by words, silence, body percussion sounds and rhythmic and non-rhythmic vocal noises. The first half of the dance ends with the sounds of the syllables of 'ma' 'nip' 'pul' 'lat' 'in' 'mot' 'tion' emerging from a cacophony of weird vocal noises.

The dance is divided into two parts by a costume change performed on stage. In between costumes Booth seems almost to stop performing and talks to the audience as if in shedding his costume he also sheds his role. He tells us about an injury he recently received to his left arm and how it will impede his dancing, at the same time giving a potted history of other injuries his body has received.

The second half of the performance begins and ends with Booth patting out rhythms on his thighs and chest. Many of the statements

---

1. The three performances of *Manipulatin' Motion (Pictures)* seen by the author took place in a theatre, a school hall and a gymnasium. The work has been performed in a variety of venues. Its improvisatory nature often results in considerable differences between performances, but it is clear that a central core of components and relations remain that give the dance its unique and recognisable character and meaning.

he makes are in the form of riddles. For example, he says 'It is in airport departure lounges', 'lovers fear it', 'It is under the bridge where the gypsies live'. The riddles are interspersed with further talk of refugees and immigrants and their journeys from south to north and back and the differences between north and south. There is also a brief interlude when he tells of memories of his childhood when his father died. Some of the words are directly related to the movements being performed. He describes a stunt in a Buster Keaton film – a house falls on Keaton but miraculously he is saved because an open window falls over his head. Booth demonstrates as he talks, letting a step ladder fall over his head, narrowly missing it so that he ends up with his head between the rungs. Other statements made relate to the technical elements of the performance, such as when he says 'cut' and at the same time the lights are turned off. He also intermittently asks questions such as 'where was I?', 'is this a story?' 'how much time have I got left?'.

The movements, like the sounds and words, cover a range from natural, everyday walking and running to more stylised gestures. The latter include backward arm circling and twisting and turning the legs and hips, both standing and on the floor, to pull the body into rolls and spirals. This technical virtuosity and skill increases as the twists and turns develop into hops and jumps and stretches on the floor. Falls are performed almost in mid-air, just caught at the last moment before imminent collapse. The quality changes when 'folksey' step patterns creep in amongst the bigger, writhing, circular movements. As the dance evolves the relationship of accompaniment to movements develops and the movements become an accompaniment to the words and sound rather than the reverse.

The performance space is lit by a standing spotlight and an anglepoise lamp clamped to a chair set downstage right on a square of newspaper. The chair has a change of costume and a towel hanging over it and a jug of water and a glass on the newspaper beside it. This area is used at 'half-time' for the costume change and Booth repairs to it occasionally to mop himself down or have a drink. He uses the whole space but frequently returns to certain areas such as the upstage left corner. This is where he ends the dance, facing the audience (after walking backwards), softening and slowing down the speed of his chest– and thigh-patting percussion as he makes his final statement before the lights fade: 'Its in a joke and I've forgotten the punch line'.

171

When analysing dance it is important to see it and its subject matter in the context of the socio-cultural background in which it is performed and/or made. In *Manipulatin' Motion (Pictures)* part of the subject matter is the plight of refugees and immigrants and the economic differences between the technologically advanced northern hemisphere and the 'underdeveloped' southern hemisphere. Other subject matter includes the object of the riddle, which appears to be death, and notions of art and theatre, performance and audience, dance and cinema which are repeatedly alluded to in the form and content of the piece and the title, *Manipulatin' Motion (Pictures)*.

The relevant values of the socio-cultural background of Britain in the early 1980s are contained in prevalent attitudes to the plight of refugees and the north/south divide. Britain is firmly in the north and most people are only occasionally concerned with the lot of refugees or those living in the southern hemisphere. This puts the dance in a certain context. So does the fact that death is regarded as a taboo topic in our culture, and art, theatre, cinema and dance are generally appreciated as sources of rich, aesthetic, cultural and/or entertainment value.

Manipulatin' Motion (Pictures) appears in a theatre context where the notion of performance in front of an audience is respected and the function or purpose of the dance is to present a significant statement or meaning in an aesthetic and entertaining manner. Booth continually exposes the performance context, pushing it to the edge of its boundaries so that the distance between audience and dancer is forever changing and the context becomes part of the content and subject matter of the dance.

Recognised criteria of excellence, norms and standards for new dance have yet to be established. A characteristic feature, sometimes claimed to be a criterion of avant garde art and new dance, has been identified as the rejection of established tradition and conventions of other styles and genres. The subject matter of the avant garde is sometimes associated with radical, social or political issues and some new dance exemplifies this. This is the context for analysis.

Manipulatin' Motion (Pictures) demonstrates and creates alternative values to those predominantly held. The subject matter contains radical, social and political elements. The treatment of the subject matter, however, needs to be considered for a fuller analysis and evaluation.

Three possible major strands of subject matter have been identified as 'refugees and immigrants', 'death', and 'the nature of
performance in the arts of theatre, dance and film'.

The relative importance of the three strands fluctuates throughout
the dance but that of 'refugees and immigrants' is underlined
because Booth mentions it before anything else, it is repeated
throughout the dance and it is presented in a more direct and
detailed manner than the other two areas. Booth states 'since the
performance began about half an hour ago on an average day about
a hundred and fifty people will have become refugees' and 'between
this movement [he moves] and this movement [he moves again] a
further five people will have become refugees'. He is using his
privilege as a performer with an attentive audience and employing
the dance medium (his excuse for being there and the context in
which he is working) to make a verbal statement about his subject
matter. In so doing he is highlighting particular moments in relation
to the linear development of the dance. This is done in an unconventional manner because the dance movements, traditionally the core
of choreography, do not appear to be important – they are almost
cast aside. He actually says at one point 'between this movement
and the one performed five minutes from now (let's imagine five
minutes have passed and the movement has been performed) approximately twenty five more people will have become refugees'. Within
an avant garde style this unconventional treatment is appropriate
especially as it serves the purpose of emphasing particular meanings
associated with the subject matter.

Another direct link between the subject matter and movements in
the dance and the nature of performance art occurs when Booth
describes the refugees, saying:

> hoards and hoards of people moving . . . moving . . . mov-
> ing . . . moving . . . I think we're being moved. I suspect
> that I'm being moved.

First the migration of the refugees is described as 'people moving',
then as Booth repeats the word 'moving' whilst he is moving it seems
simply to describe the nature of the performance he is engaged in.
Then as he states 'I think we're being moved' he seems to be saying
something about the character and purpose of art, i.e. to 'move'
people, and finally 'I suspect that I'm being moved' seems to imply
manipulation of some sort; a more devious and possibly ideological

form of influence. The way in which the components of Booth's movements and his spoken words are related in the choreography allows for a variety of unusual and unconventional interpretations which nevertheless stem from and powerfully enhance the statement about the refugees.

The second area of subject matter – the solution to the riddle – seems to be death, since towards the end of the dance Booth finishes a series of statements about the unknown 'it' with 'you cannot be immune to this so accordingly the prospect of death does not alarm me'. Right after this, Booth continues, saying 'I've considered the Washington connection, I've considered the Moscow connection' (possibly bringers of death), 'I've considered the north/south connection. It may happen forty years from now.' (presumably his own death) 'It could have happened tonight'. These statements neatly link up the three major subject areas: 'death', 'the north/south connection' and 'it could have happened tonight' – 'the performance'. Thus the three strands of subject matter are finally related in the choreography giving a sense of unity. The relations between these strands of aural elements when seen in relation to the total dance form are major relations.

There are various other references to the object of the riddle throughout the piece. Apart from the more obvious clues such as 'It is in a bullet in South Africa' and 'It is in an island in the South Atlantic,[1] other components, strands or sections of the choreography seem to allude to death. For example, at one point, from the jumble of vocal noises Booth is making, the muffled phrase 'coming up for air' can just be distinguished sounding almost like a last breath. Booth mentions his father's death and the various accidents and injuries he himself has experienced, some of which seem to be scrapes with death. When he says 'How much longer have I got?', which he repeats two or three times at different intervals, it seems to be laying bare the technical production of the dance, illustrating the nature of theatre and art, which only last for a fixed period of time, as well as his time left to live. As with the 'refugees' theme, sometimes the 'death' theme can be detected in the movements performed. For example, when he is demonstrating the Keaton stunt he takes a risk with his own body.

---

1. This statement was included in a performance at the time of the war between Britain and Argentina over the Falkland Islands.

All these reference points fit into the choreographic form of the dance. Some, such as the clues to the riddle, are repeated exactly or in a slightly altered form and become established. Others, such as 'How much longer have I got?', are repeated exactly at strategic moments in the linear development of the dance, giving the audience and Booth himself landmarks; reminders that performance is a finite event. These components and relations between them combine effectively with the riddles of the subject matter and the overall character of the dance.

The third area of subject matter, the nature of performance art in theatre, cinema and dance, is possibly less obvious than the other two but more pervasive since it is implicitly present in the whole performance. It is exemplified in Booth's varying relationship with his audience, which is evident in the movement components, aural elements and the relations between them.

The performance of movements and the sounds/words operate on a number of levels. For example, the motley of odd, vocal noises, from which the sounds of 'manipulatin' motion' gradually emerge, seems to be an almost involuntary, uncontrollable outpouring accompanied by similarly haphazard twitching, reflex movements. The next level seems to be that of natural, everyday movements and talking. During the periods when Booth uses this more straightforward approach, he often inserts reminders that the performance is still going on – when he freezes his actions in the middle of taking off a slipper or his shirt, for example. Therefore, just as the distance between audience and performer is being reduced it is abruptly widened again. These moments of stillness are repeated throughout the dance giving it a recognisable form and providing relations between these moments and the linear development of the dance.

The next level of structure appears to be the use of ambiguity and double meaning. Certain phrases, such as those concerned with 'movement' and 'being moved' (see p.173), demonstrate this. This treatment of subject matter is consistent with the riddle form of many statements and with the idea of a joke in the last two sentences of the dance: 'It's in a joke which I didn't get. It's in a joke and I've forgotten the punch line'.

Throughout the dance Booth's performance style creates an impression of teasing playfulness. The riddles, puns, the risks he takes with his body all seem to be testing the audience, seeing just how far the notions of performance and art can be stretched. Other levels of presentation are evident in the more formal, poetic deliverance of the statements about refugees and immigrants and the more skilled and stylised dance and T'ai Chi-like movements removed from the everyday walking and running with which they are interspersed. Even though these movements are more stylised the treatment remains abstract; the movement does not appear to refer to anything other than itself, focussing on its own form and level of presentation. It is manipulated motion which might be regarded as the core of the dance. Thus form and content cohere providing the dance's character and meaning.

Cinema is also about motion and this appears to be a subsidiary theme of the work. The Buster Keaton story, the cinema riddles – 'it is in cinema' and 'Cinema deals in it' – and the statement that Booth's father was a film-maker are obvious references at one level. Other references appear to expose the nature of the medium, showing the audience something of film 'behind the scenes'; for example, Booth uses technical terms and phrases such as 'cut' and 'testing 1,2,3,4'. This exposure of the 'tricks of the trade' is reinforced in the account of the Buster Keaton stunt when the audience is told that the shot which is 'forty five seconds long took three days to set up' and that a bed which is 'scuttling down the street is probably pulled by a wire we can't see'. Despite this revelation, it is apparently not intended to convey disrespect for the medium, since these statements are juxtaposed with others such as 'It is one of the greatest moments of cinema', and Keaton is described as 'my hero' and 'the most complete artist of the century'.

Although the arts of cinema, theatre and dance are in some sense totally demystified in the performance they are shown to be useful tools for conveying messages, which is why they each need their techniques and conventions. Booth seems to be exposing these for what they are, so that they do not become all-important, as in some traditional genres and styles where they replace the significance of statements and meanings expressed. As in Early's *Michael*, the form of the dance is not allowed to displace or overpower the subject matter and become the meaning and ultimate interpretation of the work.

The treatment of subject matter makes *Manipulatin' Motion (Pictures)* a highly structured and formed dance. This is reinforced by the relations between the movement components. Certain movements are repeated exactly, for example when Booth raises his right arm and stands with his back to the audience. This image is reiterated by a projection of a shadow of the arm on the back wall. He also repeats this facing in a different direction, altering the spatial element. In another example he plays with distance from the audience. Often he is at the back of the space with his back to the audience but he also uses all the space in between and at times comes quite close, facing them.

In evaluating the dance it is necessary to determine whether this tightly structured form is appropriate in relation to the subject matter, style and genre. The form appears effective in relation to the subject matter since repetition is used to establish important elements of meaning, and the dance movements, even if they do not emphasise or reinforce the meaning directly, do not detract from it. They could be said to underline it indirectly by appearing incidental compared with the words. In terms of the style of new dance a tightly formed piece may seem inappropriate since, if any criteria and norms do exist, the break with form, convention and tradition could be one of them. However, the formalism of *Manipulatin' Motion (Pictures)* is exposed in the work. It is not mystified in a conventional, traditional manner. The audience is not only allowed to see the mechanisms that hold the piece together but they are actually pointed out to them: 'How much longer have I got?', 'Is this a story?', 'Cut'. In this sense Booth is extending the boundaries of the medium in a way which is appropriate in relation to the style. The treatment of subject matter is similarly unconventional because the words are elevated instead of the movement. The content and meaning of art is thus apparently emphasised over and above its aesthetic form although it is precisely the form of the dance that subtly gives it meaning. Inasmuch as values of a recent style such as new dance are known, the choreography of *Manipulatin' Motion (Pictures)* seems appropriately and effectively to demonstrate and create these values.

The performance exhibits some features which might be termed characteristic of new dance in employing improvisation. For example, in one performance Booth feels along a ledge with his hand, stating 'This is a ledge and this is where the people fall off. This is a cliff top'. This was a new element not present in other performances of this dance. An improvisatory style was evident and also consistent with the meaning of the dance since it incorporated appropriate subject matter. The ledge reference, for example, might be alluding yet again to death.

177

The method used to analyse *Manipulatin' Motion (Pictures)* was chosen because of the nature of the dance. The aural elements of the piece appeared in some senses more important than the visual or movement components in their role as signifiers of the subject matter of the dance. Consequently, the analysis focussed on the subject matter of the dance as evident in the content of *Manipulatin' Motion (Pictures)*, which was often most apparent in the verbal statements within it.

Approaches to new dance

The difficulties of defining new dance have been adumbrated in the introduction to this chapter and accepted as a challenge. Two examples of work recognised as new dance have been chosen to represent problems that may be encountered and dealt with through dance analysis when considering new, avant garde or experimental pieces.

Before considering common features and similarities it is important to recognise the clear differences that exist between the works. For example, the movement components of *Michael* are imbued with elements of various genres and styles such as ballet and folk dance. In contrast those of *Manipulatin' Motion (Pictures)* are not derived from established dance styles, the only stylistic feature being the resemblance of some sections of movement to T'ai Chi, a martial art rather than dance. Another difference is in the use of the theatrical context. Early employs complex combinations of traditional theatrical components, such as scenery, costumes and props, to create a work of dance *theatre* and this is maintained by the distance he keeps from his audience. Booth, on the other hand, does not create an elaborate theatre context although the nature of performance seems important to him and he continually changes and plays with the distance between himself and his audience. Another difference arises in consequence of the personal relationship between performer and subject matter in *Michael*. The dance has a strong emotional quality which is absent in *Manipulatin' Motion (Pictures)*.

Despite clear differences in character certain similarities can be identified. In both dances the treatment of subject matter is such that aural elements, particularly words and statements, tend to be more important than movement at times. Both dances have intricate webs of relations that give them highly structured and complex

178

forms. In each case formal devices are exposed, for example when costumes are changed on stage. Similarly, both performers seem to be distancing themselves from their role as performers. This, like that of the weighting of aural elements over and above movement, seems to be questioning certain traditional values about the nature of art and dance. As well as the values of the art context those of the socio-cultural background are also challenged in both works by the choice of subject matter and its treatment.

These similarities exist but can they be claimed as distinctive features of new dance? Articles in early issues of *New Dance* give every indication that those involved do not necessarily see new dance in terms of a particular genre or style. For example,

> it is important that the words 'new dance' do not become a label for a certain type of work which appears to belong to a small clique of artists . . . There is no one way of working or type of work that can be labelled 'new dance'.
>
> Claid (1977, p.2)

However, there are indications that new dance does have certain broad aims that characterise it. In the first issue of *New Dance*, Jacky Lansley, one of the editors, states that,

> inherent in much of the work is an attempt to break through restrictive categorisation into a flexible way of working that does not limit one to the use of a few specialised skills and formulas.
>
> Lansley (1977, p.3)

The exploration of 'new ground' (*ibid.*) seems to be a common feature of the work, as is its needs for new criteria and terminology. Indeed, it is the continuing attempt to categorise and interpret new dance using inappropriate criteria that is the basis for Crickmay's complaint, quoted in the introduction to this chapter, that new dance as seen from a traditional standpoint remains invisible; he does, however, give a clue to a solution.

> The work differs from traditional dance forms in seeking continually to overturn habits of response and perception.
>
> Crickmay (1982, p.8)

In the above analyses of Booth's and Early's work we noted that they seem to be aiming to do just this. In this sense some new dance works seem to have elements in common, often bound up with their choice of subject matter and its treatment rather than any distinctive movement features. It is difficult to locate any specific criteria or values of the work other than, perhaps, iconoclasm itself.

Lack of definition of genre and style of new dance presents certain problems for analysis. However, these problems do not render analysis impossible as long as they are recognised and attempts are *not* made to categorise new dance within inappropriate existing genres or styles.

In the introduction to this chapter we suggest that application of an analytical framework to new dance may raise questions. However, as Lansley said in the first issue of *New Dance* itself,

> dance like any other art form does not exist within a social or intellectual vacuum . . . We can never exclude thought from our practice. Any 'live' situation, however abstract in content, is still a momentary glance at a vast history of ideas and gestures which are open to analysis and interpretation.

> Lansley (1977, p.3)

CHAPTER 10

Further applications for dance analysis in theory and practice

by Janet Adshead and Pauline Hodgens

Subtle variations in interpretations of *Swan Lake; Dark Elegies* seen as a dance specifically of its time in one sense, yet transcending its period of origin in another; the immediacy of Booth's and Early's work and its capacity for social statement – these examples (Chapters 7, 8 and 9) serve to indicate some of the possibilities of a systematic approach to the appreciation of dance. They show analysis to be a positive force in generating enjoyment and understanding of dance in performance, enjoyment which is heightened by an awareness of nuances of expression.

The value of analysis rests on this capacity to give access to the dance, to enable the choreographer, the dancer and the spectator to see clearly and to make sense of what is seen. 'Making sense' would be limited if it remained at the level of generalisations about the meaning of the dance or its qualities without reference to the detail of the movement and the structure of the dance, since it is this that ultimately supports and substantiates any statement of the character of the dance, or reference to its aesthetic qualities. Conversely, attention given only to the detail of movement and structure without reference to qualities and meanings would be equally if differently limited.

In this final chapter it is pertinent to return to some of the notions outlined in Chapter 1 in the light of the intervening chapters. The development of a sound theoretical framework for the analysis of dances was identified as the primary objective. It can be seen that identifying the principles on which a systematic method of analysis relies is a complex matter and one which requires further elucidation than can be given in an introductory account.

A theory of dance analysis, it was argued, would have to make reference to existing theories derived both from other arts and from the other contexts in which dances occur, that is, from the art theory world as much as from anthropological studies. A sketch of such a theory is outlined in Chapters 2–5 but a more extensive exploration of the nature of the relationship between analytical frameworks in dance, drama, literature, the visual arts and music would offer further insights.

One of the apparent deficiencies in the world of dance is the lack of a substantial literature which deals with the dance works themselves. The other arts appear to have no such problem since scholarly and detailed analyses, explanations and discussions abound. If dance is to gain and maintain a credible position amongst the arts, then scholars must take its artefacts more seriously and show themselves capable of working at depth. There is certainly a growing desire amongst a rapidly increasing student and scholar population for a more critical and investigatory consideration of dance, a concern which motivated this particular text. The authors are anxious to see and contribute to a growth in analytical, scholarly and critical writing and debate on dance. Thus, the aim is to establish both a critical *procedure* and a sound, underlying critical *theory* so that this kind of work can be approached systematically at the simplest and earliest level (i.e. in schools) and continue and develop through to postgraduate and postdoctoral level.

Critical procedures and theories exist in relation to other art forms and while they are not necessarily relevant and appropriate for the study of dance they may make important contributions and highlight significant considerations. The authors, aware of these particular theories and procedures, but unwilling to adopt them uncritically, began the search for the fundamental principles embodied within this text from two different, but eventually merging, points. These were, firstly, a detailed appraisal of many dance works and, secondly, a scrutiny of a variety of terms, topics, issues and problems (often philosophical in nature) generated by dance and dances. The clarification which arose from both lines of investigation has created the foundations for what we see to be a workable critical method supported by a serious and substantial theory. However, a great deal more research needs to be done in both conceptual and empirical modes in order to build upon this initial foundation.

Many of the concepts dealt with in the preceding chapters need further elucidation and expansion; there is neither enough detail to encourage and sustain the discussion and debate which must ensue, nor sufficient scholarly work to provide the basis for any general agreement amongst those interested. For instance, there is little agreed use for the terms the dance world so readily employs.

The notion of 'style' is a good example of an unclear and ubiquitous term. To talk of Twyla Tharp's or Michael Clark's style might be a reference to their (equally uninhibited) attitude to, and selection of, movement; or to the structural or choreographic devices used in creating form (through fugue or types of repetition); or to an idiosyncratic method of treating subject matter (for example, the violence of human relationships found in Tharp's *Bad Smells* or Clark's *New Puritans*); or to an apparently casual manner of performance. The term is also used with reference to common characteristics of a nation, company or group. Across the arts 'genre' sometimes replaces 'style' and stands for similar notions, in other instances it identifies larger categories than the notion of style.

In all the arts the process of categorising and classifying examples of works is important, not merely as an academic exercise, but to reveal fundamental facts which are often assumed or ignored. The discernment of important common characteristics or significant differences amongst art works is the first step towards identifying the basic choreographic concerns or interests shared across a number of works and the choreographic methods employed to deal with them. The concerns and interests evident in a group of works point directly to the differing or common values and beliefs of the time, the place and the choreographers. They expose underlying and common rules and reveal the less specific conventions and traditions which are assumed or employed. A study of the complete works of any choreographer, for instance MacMillan, would reveal how one particular person has approached and used the materials and ideas traditionally associated with the form of dance within which he creates; what his values and beliefs are and how they may differ from those of other choreographers; which rules he acknowledges, rejects or bends; how he has responded to the traditions and conventions of the form and in what sense he may have created a distinctive style of his own.

This kind of consideration, taken over a large range of examples of different kinds of dance and different choreographers, reveals how the art form as a whole has changed, developed and diversified and how and why dance is what it is at the present time. Further studies of this kind, conducted in depth, are the next stage of research.

In the same way the notions of 'subject matter' and 'treatment' require further amplification. It is not immediately obvious what is meant by these terms and how they relate to those of 'content', 'topic', 'source' or 'stimulus'. The terms most frequently and loosely used to refer to the treatment of subject matter are those of 'lyrical', 'abstract', 'dramatic' or 'narrative' modes. If this kind of terminology can be clarified then the enquiry can be expanded to consider how the specific set of conventions and 'rules' transform the subject matter to create identifiable genres and styles.

It would be interesting to know, from a detailed examination of dance works, which kinds of subject matter typify periods within a choreographer's life and within certain styles of dance. Some such studies have been undertaken on some of the major figures of modern dance, e.g. Martha Graham, and generalisations about her choreography in terms of an 'American period', or 'Greek myth' style, or the recurrence of psychological dramas as subject matter, are the result. Scholarly study would seek to demonstrate from the *dance*, not simply from its title and the external narrative *from which it derives, what* is dealt with and *how* this is done. The relationship between a style of dance (for instance the particular collection of characteristics that made early British ballet of the 1930s such a growing force) and the subject matter of the dances is not simple.

If terms such as 'post punk expressionism', 'neoclassical abstraction' and 'romantic modernism' have some valid use they may be pointers to the choreographic concerns of a person or a period. For the spectator, relating one work to another by means of such categories may also provide an entry to difficult works.

This kind of debate leads directly to considerations of 'materials' and 'form', for different kinds of dance have characteristic selections of materials and different ways of structuring that which is used. Descriptions of the basic material of movement raise terminological problems about the appropriate vocabulary for such descriptions and, indeed, the possibility and desirability of generating a common language for all of the phenomena known as dance.

Closely allied is the problem of how this movement material is structured, in the dance as a whole and in relation to the other components, raising similar questions pertaining to form and structural devices. For instance, certain selections of movements and devices for structuring dances may be found to typify a particular period or place in dance history and, if this is the case, understanding how and why they have assumed such importance is crucial. If specific characteristics can be isolated then it is possible both to trace developments from period to period or place to place and to identify those selections and structures central to the larger groups of works known as genres or styles.

In relation to the individual choreographer the use of a limited or greater range of possibilities and the way preferences relate to the genre or style within which s/he works is of considerable interest. It is valid to study the work of Robert Cohan, for instance, and to ask how the movement selection and structural devices he employees relate to those of Martha Graham from whom his work derives; how his own choreography has developed in these two respects from the mid 1960s to the present day; whether there is any consistency in that which he selects and employs and therefore whether or not his inimitable style is characterised by one or both of these factors. This would produce a more considered view of his work than is currently available.

None of these topics are easy to deal with either conceptually or in a more investigatory or empirical mode. They are elusive but it is also apparent from the preceding discussions that they are tied together in a web of relationships which create further complications. They need to be approached separately but with constant reference to each other. Until they are investigated in this way we can hardly be sure about what kinds of questions we need to ask or what in the end may be revealed. However, it is also the case that they are embedded in considerations which are far more extensive and fundamental. For instance, they relate directly to problems of 'meaning'. This notion raises a series of serious questions such as whether or not it is appropriate to say that dances mean something, how dances mean things, how we know the meanings and whether dance functions as a language or a number of languages – literally or analogously.

The meaning or significance of any individual dance relates to and rests upon a variety of factors. The traditions, conventions, rules, norms and values of each genre and style govern how and what any dance within its aegis may mean or signify. Dances are approached or 'read' through the relevant conventions and expectations; in this sense meaning is both genre, and style-dependent and specific. However, once the nature or type of dance has been established then the meaning may be arrived at through taking two different approaches. In the first place meaning is derived directly in relation to the text or the work itself. In the terms already used, it is the further consideration of the subject matter, the form of treatment adopted, the selection, nature and use of the components and the choice and use of structural devices which reveal the detailed meaning of the work. If we were to consider Cohan's *Stabat Mater* (1975) in this way, that is, to make an interpretation of the work, we would undoubtedly wish to attend to components such as the number and role of the dancers, the costume, set and light, the music and the wide variety of movement. Each of these is significant and together they create particular effects, moods or atmospheres. Although these may give substantial information about the work, it is not until we have penetrated the form of the work that interpretative statements can be made in their full depth and detail. The fact that this work falls into two major parts, has three sections and nine subsections is particularly significant, for these divisions and units reveal the changing and developing mood of the work through stages from anguish to a final acceptance or hope. The use of solos, trios and the group and the careful interplay of these relationships reveal other facets of meaning pertaining specifically to 'Mary's' developing insight and understanding. The perception of various images, allusions and symbols such as the cross, the crown, the spears and the trinity or triangle all cast light and inform the more subtle levels of meaning of the piece.

However, it may also be the case that meaning is attributed to the work because of certain contextual information, information which illuminates, draws attention to, or amplifies the text in some way. In the particular instance of *Stabat Mater* it may be that, for example, the biblical account of the crucifixion, or of Mary's involvement with her son, or of events in the lives of the other Marys of the gospel, or a careful study of the sung poem may inform the 'reading'. Knowledge of the effects for which Cohan was striving may similarly guide our perception and understanding of the work. (For an expanded debate on *Stabat Mater* see articles by Hodgens (1987) and by Messenger (1987) on the choreographic and musical structures of the piece.) This raises a very serious issue about the relevance and role of contextual (sometimes called extrinsic) information in the reading of any art work. Debates abound on the autonomy or dependence of the art work, the freedom and constraints of the spectator, and the role and relationship of the artist to the art work.

More extensive considerations of meaning could take us into a study of any one choreographer's approach. We may discern whether s/he uses certain methods of conveying meaning so often that they indicate a consistency across her/his work and whether these characteristics are shared by other choreographers working in the same genre or style. One may ask whether or not genres and styles themselves embody characteristic ways of conveying meaning. For instance we know that, broadly speaking, dances may be representational or non-representational; whether any of the genres or styles we can identify *rest* upon this distinction is an interesting question. Taking extremes, does ballet, for instance, use predominantly representational methods for conveying meaning and is post-modern dance mainly in a mode which is non-representational? Another line of enquiry pertains to these two notions themselves. If dances are representational, what devices or methods are used by choreographers? One might examine how in *La Fille mal gardee* Ashton employs literal movement and mime to convey farmyard animals, human personality and character, thoughts about future marriage and family, atmosphere, events, and love and how this relates to other non-literal devices.

If dance is seen as non-representational, questions of meaning still remain since dances are not meaning*less* although the meaning may be obscure or the point of the work better described in terms of its 'significance'. In relation to these dances the notions of symbolism, imagery and allusion are perhaps more appropriate and require further exploration. In the pursuit of meaning in dance some of the major terms such as communication, expression, symbolism, representation also require investigation and explanation in the light of current theory in aesthetics, semiotics etc. Debates on topics such as the autonomy of art, the artist's intention and aesthetic involvement appear as further key issues in aesthetics.

It has been said that theories and procedures developed in relation to the other arts have not been adopted wholesale but nevertheless these investigations have proceeded with constant reference to them. Theory in aesthetics, literature (particularly structuralism and semiotics) and formal musical analysis have informed the writing and assisted in the location of principles, terminology and procedures for the critical approach to dance adopted in this text.

The kind of work which has been stressed so far is that of a conceptual nature but this is not enough nor can it be isolated. It is important that from this rigorous kind of search or debate comes a desire and ability to engage in the practical and painstaking work of analysing dances. This develops scholarship in a number of ways, giving rise to analyses in written form, critiques and discussions of methods and procedures of analysis and of the dances themselves, debates on groups of works such as schools or styles, and writings on the relevance, application or illumination of those issues already investigated in the more conceptual mode. Discussion and debate, argument and counter-argument are central to the development of any art and to the growing understanding of the potential audience.

For an analytic framework to be of any value it must prove itself in application in particular circumstances by particular people and here we raise again some of the many possibilities but now in the light of the arguments put forward earlier.

The *choreographer*, or maker of the dance, selects and structures dance components for the purpose of presenting a dance which has specific character, quality and meaning. The selection and structuring of movement is determined by considerations of the genre, style and subject matter of the dance and the way in which the choreographer intends to treat it. These interrelated factors determine both what is possible and what is appropriate in the creation of a particular dance. In the process of making the dance the choreographer assesses, diagnoses and changes or amends aspects of the dance, i.e. the components or the form, either because the dance does not bring into being the right character and quality and thus the type or shade of meaning desired, or because it does not create something which has worth in the choreographer's eyes. This requires an essentially analytic act of judgement combined with imaginative engagement with the work.

The *dancer's* concern is with the mastery of the technical demands and with interpretation in order that the spectator can grasp the meaning and appreciate the worth of the dance. Dancers have to understand how to achieve this and, therefore, they necessarily employ a (more or less explicit) form of analysis.

Although the choreographer and performer are concerned with the skills and concepts identified in this text they may work successfully without a *direct* use for them beyond recognising that some kind of an analytic process occurs. Analysis is more obviously useful to anyone who wishes to *understand* the work of the choreographer and performer, and in the *education* of choreographers and performers. In preparing the dancer or the emergent choreographer it is vitally important, if they are to work intelligently, that they come to understand the procedures and processes that typify the choreographic act and the appraisals made by appreciators of their work.

To this end the choreographer and performer are important *spectators* of their own work although the audience for dance is of course much wider than this. Some may watch simply in order to enjoy and appreciate while certain 'specialist' types of spectator can also be identified, notably the director, the reconstructor, the notator, the critic, the historian, sociologist, etc.

The *director* of a performance makes decisions concerning the overall character of a production, the performance style and the set, the use of costume and other, more practical, matters. In the revival of classical works and, more recently, of early modern dance works, reconstruction skills may also be necessary, entailing the interpretation of a notated score and production of the work in the light of previously existing performances.

Choreographers' notes, video and film allow comparisons across a number of works by the same choreographer, from which the director or reconstructor may come to certain conclusions about a choreographer's habitual ways of dealing with movement. However, this can only be deduced by much wider reading than that of the score and by taking cognisance of contemporary sources such as descriptions of the dance from those who watched and performed it.

The question of style reappears here in a complex form since the director or reconstructor needs to take account of the individual choreographer's general style; the style of the particular work; the style of that genre or form of dance; and the style of that period, country, and 'school' of dance within a national style. Creating an authentic reconstruction clearly rests on the recognition that the meaning and value of the dance reside in certain features and that these cannot be changed without the dance losing its integrity. But, if museum pieces are not to be the result, the director also needs to be aware that the classics in any performing art survive partly *because* they are constantly reinterpreted. Valid reconstructions in this case would be impossible without careful, analytic study.

Notators also reconstruct, but as a prior act they are instrumental in getting the dance down on paper as it was created. The notator's major problem lies in deciding which aspects of the dance are structural components, and hence integral to the choreography, and which are matters of interpretation. The notation system itself helps here since it will normally distinguish between observable features of movement, design, rhythm, etc. and expressive qualities, or instructions to perform in a certain manner, which give rise to the performer's interpretation of the piece.

The *critic*, supposedly the most detached of all spectators from the process of making or performing the dance, uses analysis combined with extensive socio-historical or other biographical and cultural background material in order to evoke the dance in literary terms and thereby to inform, to educate, to interpret, to appraise and to evaluate works of art.

The critic does this in relation to the structure of the choreography; the processes of making (if these are accessible and relevant); the particular performance witnessed (possibly in comparison with other performances); individual dancers' strengths and weaknesses etc. What the use of an analytic procedure can provide is a system which underpins this so that the reader can at least agree or disagree on the basis of the reasons offered rather than absorbing opinion masquerading as fact.

Historical accounts of dance tend to describe circumstances surrounding the dance, events in which it played a part, costumes worn, etc., and while this is both a valuable and a legitimate activity, it is one in which the dance may become obscure. In the initial stages analysis can provide a framework within which separate fragments can be fitted together to gain a more or less complete picture of the dance. Subsequently the analytic procedure can be used on the assembled information. It generates a way of looking for the dance in a mass of historical material, i.e. searching out its characteristic movement features, the way in which the movements are put together, the kinds of interpretations proffered at the time, the reasons given for them and evaluations that have been made of the dance since its first performances. The relevance of analysis for the sociologist or anthropologist parallels that described for the historian. Any investigator who starts from a standpoint or discipline outside the dance has the dual problem of remaining true to that discipline and also true to an investigation of dance.

In conclusion, analysis of dances is embryonic at the present time. It is open to criticism on the one hand from choreographers and performers fearful of the destruction of their art and, on the other, from some academics looking for their own methodology (for example, of literary criticism, musicology and anthropology). With more justification, perhaps, other academics may search for a new methodology at a level of sophistication equal to that found in parallel disciplines. Specialists in any one aspect of dance analysis, perhaps in Labananalysis or ethnomusicology, may search in vain for the insights of their own discipline. What we seek is the depth of the discipline of *dance*, starting from the elements that characterise it uniquely and that derive from its internal structure. Dance is not simply movement (to be understood solely by analysing it in these terms, whether through Laban's concepts or biomechanical factors), it is not simply another way of relating a story (to be understood by applying narrative theory), it is not simply an interesting extension of musical practice (to be understood by techniques of musical analysis) and it is not only a reflection of mid twentieth-century behaviour (to be understood through psychoanayltic theory). Its methodologies are likely to share these other approaches only if dances are illuminated by them. The obverse is to force dance into an alien framework, shaping it to another mould designed for another purpose.

By means of this text we aim to contribute to the debate about analysis and to the development of an analytic tradition in dance while being aware of the apprehension that this may generate. We hope to persuade, by illustration, explanation and argument, that this is not an activity which threatens a love of dance but one that deepens it, guiding the observer to a more profound knowledge and sensitivity. Perception is heightened and all the spectator's faculties, knowledge and previous experiences of dance are then brought face to face with the dance.

The authors' interest in the area lies in the extent to which this depth of appreciation can be made explicit. We argue that there are many skills that can be learnt, knowledge that can be imparted and much work that can be undertaken to aid the imaginative process of appreciation.

This is essentially an educational endeavour (in the widest sense) and, pertinently, it is the development of dance in the educational system and the work of recent pioneers in the development of new curricula which has stimulated this analytic work. The shared traditions, but distinctively different degrees of progress among the arts, indicate that dance has a long way to go. This text is directed at serious students of dance, at the teacher and researcher and at the critic. It should not be mistaken for a reviewer's guide or for a handbook of analysis – it is an exploration of the problems of analysis and an attempt to draw together theoretical structures which will support and guide the analysis of dances.

In constructing a theory that is so broadly based, by virtue of drawing on movement analysis, compositional theories, notation theory, philosophical aesthetics, literary and music theory, social anthropology and dance history, there is a danger of falling between too many disciplines. The vision that the authors have is of something other than simply remaining true to existing disciplines, rather we have a sense that it should be possible to unify the relevant insights from other sources into a composite theory of dance analysis since they all speak of dance and illuminate it in different ways. Overarching theories can readily be criticised for lack of depth, for lack of knowledge in particular areas, and we acknowledge that the full range of these disciplines could not be contained in an introductory text. The intention is to indicate the richness and depth of study that is now possible if the dance student draws upon these areas, removes the blinkers that sometimes tie scholars to one school of thought and focusses anew on the dance.

It is a matter of fact which can be proved by reference to the existing dance literature that very little analysis of dance takes place that is methodical and systematic. It is a matter for discussion whether it ought to, or how much of it should take place. It is our intention to share with the reader ideas about the potential value of pursuing studies of this kind.

These areas of debate and potential research, both towards conceptual clarification and in the substantiation of theoretical frameworks through extensive study of the works, genres and styles, offer a programme for dance research well into the twenty-first century.

References

Chapter 1

Adorno, T W, 1982 'On the problem of musical analysis'. *Musical Analysis* Vol.1 no. 2, July, pp. 169–88

Adshead, J, 1980 'Dance as a discipline'. University of Leeds PhD thesis

Adshead, J, 1981 *The study of dance*, London: Dance Books

Adshead, J, and Hetherington, M, 1987 *Directory of dance courses in higher education*, National Resource Centre for Dance: Standing Conference on Dance in Higher Education

Adshead, J, Briginshaw, V A, Hodgens, P, and Huxley, M, 1982 'A chart of skills and concepts for dance', *The Journal of Aesthetic Education* vol. 16 no. 3, Fall, pp. 49–61

Becker, S, and Roberts, J, 1983 'A reaffirmation of the Humphrey–Weidman quality', *Dance Notation Journal* vol. 1 no. 1, pp. 3–17

Best, D, 1986 *Feeling and reason in the arts*. London: Allen and Unwin

Bissell, R, 1983 'Rooms: an analysis'. *Dance Notation Journal* vol. 1. no. 1, pp. 18–34

Daiches, D, 1981 (2nd edn) *Critical approaches to literature*. London: Longman

Hammond, S N, 1984 'Clues to ballet's technical history from the early nineteenth century ballet lesson. *Dance Research* vol. 3 no. 1, pp. 53–66

Hutchinson Guest, A, 1984 *Dance notation*. London: Dance Books

Jonas, O, 1982 *Introduction to the theory of Heinrich Schenker: the nature of the musical work of art*. New York: Longman

Smith, R A, and Smith, C M, 1977 'The artworld and aesthetic skills'. *The Journal of Aesthetic Education* vol. 11 no. 2, April, pp. 117–32

Woolf, V, 1909 'Impressions at Bayreuth'. *The Times* 21.8.1909. Republished in *Books and portraits* (1979), pp. 31–5. London: Triad/Panther

Chapters 2–5

Backman, E L, 1952 repr. 1977 *Religious dances in the Christian church and in popular medicine*. Connecticut: Greenwood

Bartenieff, I, 1967. 'Research in anthropology: a study of dance styles in primitive cultures'. *CORD Dance Research Annual I*: 'Research in dance: problems and possibilities', pp. 91–104

Bartenieff, I, Hackney, P, Jones, B T, Van Zile, J, and Wolz, C, 1984 'The potential of movement analysis as a research tool: a preliminary analysis'. *Dance Research Journal* 16/1, Spring, pp. 3–26

Best, D, 1974 'The aesthetic in sport'. *British Journal of Aesthetics* vol. 14 no. 3, pp. 197–213

Clifton, P, and Hulme, A–M, 1982 Solo step dancing within living memory in North Norfolk. *Proceedings of the first Traditional Dance Conference*, pp. 29–58. Crewe and Alsager College of Higher Education

Cohen, L R, 1978 'Introduction to Labananalysis: effort/shape'. *CORD Dance Research Annual IX*: 'Essays in dance research', pp. 53–8

Cook, R, 1977 *The dance director*. New York: Dance Notation Bureau

Croce, A, 1977 *Afterimages*. New York:Knopf

Dance Perspectives no. 34, 1968 Merce Cunningham

Davis, M A, and Schmais, C, 1967 'An analysis of the style and composition of *Water Study'*. *CORD Dance Research Annual I*, pp. 105–13

Gellerman, J, 1978 'The "Mayim" pattern as an indicator of cultural attitudes in three American Hasidic communities: a comparative approach based on Labananalysis'. *CORD Dance Research Annual IX*. pp. 111–44

Guillot, G, and Prudhommeau, G, 1976 *The book of ballet*. New Jersey: Prentice Hall

Hanna, J L, 1979 *To dance is human. A theory of non-verbal communication*. Austin: University of Texas

Hilton, W, 1981 *Dance of court and theatre. The French Noble Style 1690–1725*. London: Dance Books

Hulme, A–M, and Clifton, P, 1978 'Social dancing in a Norfolk village 1900–1945', *Folk Music Journal* vol. 3 no. 4, pp. 359–77

Humphrey, D, 1959 *The art of making dances*. New York, Grove.

Hutchinson Guest, A, 1981 *Fanny Elssler's Cachucha*. London: Dance Books

Hutchinson Guest, A, 1983 'In question: the body'. *Dance Research* vol. 1 no. 1, Spring, pp. 69–76.

Hutchinson Guest, A, 1984 *Dance notation*. London: Dance Books

Jordan, S, 1981/2 'Issues in Labananalysis research. Using the Humphrey scores'. *Dance Research Journal* vol. 14 no. 1/2, pp. 51–3

Judge, R, 1983 'Tradition and the plaited maypole dance'. *Traditional Dance* vol. 2, pp. 1-21. Crewe and Alsager College of Higher Education

Kaeppler, A L, 1971 'Aesthetics of Tongan dance'. *Ethnomusicology* vol. 15 no. 2, pp. 175–85

Kaeppler, A L, 1972 'Method and theory in analyzing dance structure with an analysis of Tongan dance'. *Ethnosmusicology* vol. 16 no. 2, pp. 173–217

Kagan, E, 1978 'Towards the analysis of a score. A comparative study of *Three Epitaphs* by Paul Taylor and *Water Study* by Doris Humphrey', *CORD Dance Research Annual IX*: 'Essays in dance research'. pp. 75–92

Kealiinohomoku, J W, 1970 'Ethnic historical study'. *CORD: Proceedings of the second conference on research in dance.* 'Dance history research: perspectives from related arts and disciplines', pp. 86–97

King, E, 1978 *Transformations: a memoir of the Humphrey–Weidman era.* New York: Dance Horizons

Laban, R, 1966 *Choreutics.* Ann/ed. Lisa Ullman. London: Macdonald & Evans

Macaulay, A, 1980 'First impressions'. *Dancing Times*, August, pp. 734–35

Manor, G, 1980 *The gospel according to dance: choreography and the bible.* New York: St. Martin's Press

Margolis, J, 1980 *Art and philosophy.* Brighton: Harvester

Najder, Z, 1975 *Values and evaluations.* Oxford: Clarendon

Percival, J, 1982 Programme note, Royal Opera House, 19 March

Pforsich, J, 1978 'Labananalysis and dance style research'. *CORD Dance Research Annual IX*: 'Essays in dance research'. pp. 59–74

Preston-Dunlop, V, 1963, 1980 *Handbook for modern educational dance.* London: Macdonald and Evans

Preston-Dunlop, V, 1983 Choreutic concepts and practice. *Dance Research* vol. 1 no. 1, Spring, pp. 77–88

Siegel, M, 1979 *The shapes of change.* Boston: Houghton Mifflin

Stearns, M, and Stearns, J, 1964 *Jazz dance.* New York: Macmillan

Walther, S, 1979 'A cross cultural approach to dance criticism'. *CORD Dance Research Annual X*, pp. 65–75

195

Wynne, S, and Woodruff, D, 1970 'Reconstruction of a dance from 1700'. *CORD Proceedings of the second conference*. 'Dance history research: perspectives from related arts and disciplines'. pp. 26–55

Chapter 6

Adshead, J, Briginshaw, V A, Hodgens, P, and Huxley, M, 1982 'A chart of skills and concepts for dance'. *The Journal of Aesthetic Education* vol. 16 no. 3, Fall, pp. 49–61

Goolsby, T, 1984 'Music education as aesthetic education: concepts and skills for the appreciation of music'. *The Journal of Aesthetic Education* vol. 18 no. 4, Winter, pp. 15–33

Smith, R A, and Smith, C M, 1977 'The artworld and aesthetic skills'. *The Journal of Aesthetic Education* vol. 11 no. 2, April, pp. 117–32

Chapter 7

Beaumont, C W, 1950 'The characters in *Swan Lake*'. *Ballet*, March, pp. 20–6

Beaumont, C W, 1952 *The ballet called Swan Lake*. London: Beaumont

Bland, A, 1981 *The Royal Ballet: the first fifty years*. London: Threshold

Clarke, M, 1963 'Fonteyn, Nureyev and dancers of the Royal Ballet'. *Dancing Times*, March, pp. 340–1

Gray, F, 1952 *Ballet for beginners*. London: Phoenix

Guest, I, 1980 'The age of Petipa', in Steinberg, C, (ed.) *The dance anthology*. New York: New American Library, pp. 374–81

Kersley, L, and Sinclair, J, 1973 (3rd edn.) *A dictionary of ballet terms*. London: A & C Black

Koegler, H, 1977 *The concise Oxford dictionary of ballet*. London: OUP

Siegel, M B, 1974 'Steps in the fog'. *Watching the dance go by* (1977), pp. 8–13. Boston: Houghton Mifflin

Slonimsky, Y, 1959 'Writings on Lev Ivanov' *Dance Perspectives* no. 2, Spring,

Swift, M, 1968 *The art of the dance in the USSR*. Paris: University of Notre Dame

Chapter 8

Anon 1937 'Duchess theatre: a Mahler ballet'. *The Times* 22 February

Anon 1969 'The first three years of "new" Rambert'. *Dancing Times*, November, pp. 84–5

Brinson, P, and Van Praagh, P, 1963 *The choreographic art*. London: A & C Black

Brinson, P, and Crisp, C, 1970 *Ballet for all: a guide to one hundred ballets*. London: Pan

Brinson, P, and Crisp, C, 1980 *Ballet and dance: a guide to the repertory*. London: David & Charles

Clarke, M, 1962 *Dancers of mercury: the story of Ballet Rambert*. London: A & C Black

Clarke, M, 1967 'Ballet Rambert – old and new'. *Dancing Times*, January, pp. 178–9

Clarke, M, 1980 'Ballet Rambert's new/old programme'. *Dancing Times*, December, p.175

Clarke, M, 1981a 'Royal Ballet at Covent Garden'. *Dancing Times*. January, pp. 238–40

Clarke, M, 1981b 'Ballet Rambert in London'. *Dancing Times*, April, pp. 454–5

Cohen, S J, 1963 'Antony Tudor, Part two: the years in America and after'. *Dance Perspectives* no. 18

Coton, A V, 1938 *A prejudice for ballet*. London: Methuen

Coton, A V, 1941–2 'Antony Tudor: an English career'. Reprinted in *Writings on dance 1938–1968* (1975), pp. 59–71. London: Dance Books

Coton, A V, 1946 *The new ballet: Kurt Jooss and his work*. London: Dobson

Crisp, C, Sainsbury, A, and Williams, P, (eds) 1976, 1981 *Ballet Rambert: fifty years and on* (2nd edn). London: Scolar

Denby, E, 1944 'Ballet Theatre's Parsifal'. Reprinted in *Looking at the dance* (1968), pp. 74–5. New York: Curtis

Dodd, C, 1969 'The return of springtime: Rambert style'. *Dancing Times*, May, pp. 407–8

Dromgoole, N, 1981 'Faceless blunders'. *Daily Telegraph*, 22 March

Goodwin, N, 1980 '*Dark Elegies*: Mahler, Tudor and the dance'. *Royal Opera House, Covent Garden, programme,* 5 December

The Grand Theatre, Leeds, 1980 'Ballet Rambert'. *Programme and magazine* vol. 5 no. 9, 25 November

Hall, F, 1950 *Modern English ballet: an interpretation*. London: Melrose

Hall, F, 1981 'Rambert v. the Royal in *Dark Elegies*'. *Daily Telegraph*, 11 March

Lloyd, M, 1949, 1970 *The Borzoi book of modern dance*. Repub. New York: Dance Horizons

Mason, N, 1972 'You can trust some things over 30: a review of American Ballet Theatre's premières and revivals'. *Dancing Times*, March, pp. 63–6

Payne, C, 1978 *American Ballet Theatre*. London: A & C Black

Percival, J, 1963 'Antony Tudor. Part one: the years in England'. *Dance Perspectives* no. 17

Percival, J, 1972 'The Dutch National Ballet at the Stadsschouwburg, Amsterdam'. *Dance and Dancers* August pp. 48–50

The Sitter Out* 1937 'Too much tap – Rambert Ballet – Uday Shankar – Argentinita'. *Dancing Times*, April, pp. 3–5

Chapter 9

Claid, E, 1977 'New dance : a definition'. *New Dance* no. 3, Summer, p.2

Crickmay, A, 1982 'The apparently invisible dances of Miranda Tufnell and Dennis Greenwood'. *New Dance* no. 21, Spring, pp. 7–8

Early, F, 1982 *Are you right there Michael are you right?* Programme

Early, F, and Lansley, J, 1981 *I, Giselle*. Programme

Lansley, J, 1977 'Writing'. *New Dance* no. 1, New Year, p.3

Woodward, I, 1981 'Playing games'. *The Sunday Times*, 18 October

Chapter 10

Hodgens, P, 1987 'The choreographic structure of Cohan's *Stabat Mater*' in Adshead, J (ed.) *Choreography: principles and practice*. Report of the fourth Study of Dance conference, University of Surrey: Dance Research Unit

Messenger, T, 1987 'The musical structure of Vivaldi's *Stabat Mater*' in Adshead, J (ed.), *Choreography: principles and practice*. Report of the fourth Study of Dance conference, University of Surrey: Dance Research Unit

NB *Dance and Dancers* was not published during the 1980–1981 season when Ballet Rambert and The Royal Ballet gave new productions of *Dark Elegies*, hence no reviews.

---

* P J S Richardson